# SPICE JOURNEY

## SHANE DELIA

**MURDOCH BOOKS**

SYDNEY · LONDON

Introduction  8

Malta  10

Lebanon  24

Iran  68

Turkey  94

# MOROCCO 162

# ANDALUCÍA
## SPAIN 214

## PANTRY 266
*pantry items are indicated
by an asterisk within recipes

## INDEX 268

## ABOUT THE AUTHOR

Shane Delia is the star of the television show *Shane Delia's Spice Journey,* and the chef and owner of Maha restaurant and Biggie Smalls kebab shop, both in Melbourne, Australia. He is a Western Bulldog Football Club, Melbourne City Football Club, Mercedes Benz Australia and charity ambassador.

Shane's cheeky personality and enthusiasm for food and culture is captured in his acclaimed television program, which has aired in 135 countries across five continents and continues to be an Australian and international success.

Shane's flagship restaurant Maha has gone from strength to strength since its inception in 2008. Renowned for its fresh, unrestricted Middle Eastern menu, Maha has a style that is truly cutting edge. *The Age Good Food Guide* has continually recognised Maha as a leader in its field, awarding the restaurant One Chef Hat annually since 2009.

Shane is based in Melbourne. His wife Maha is the inspiration and namesake of his restaurant. Together they have two children, daughter Jayda and son Jude.

This is his second book.

# INTRODUCTION

I'm sure you have been asked, 'If you were given just one wish, what would that wish be?' It's a daunting question to most people; endless possibilities run through the mind contemplating things that would otherwise be unobtainable or impossible to achieve.

For a cook who comes from a family deeply rooted in its Phoenician ancestry, who has married into a Lebanese family that lives and breathes food and humble hospitality, the ultimate wish I could ever be granted would be to explore and celebrate the food traditions of the Middle East. In 2013, I was given the opportunity to create a television cooking show, *Spice Journey*, with the Australian television station Special

Broadcasting Service (SBS), travelling across the Middle East, meeting cooks from all walks of life, discovering ancient and modern dishes and then returning home and reinterpreting them at my Melbourne restaurant, Maha. Three seasons on, seeing what I have seen, my spice journey has given me more than I could have ever wished for.

This book is the culmination of my travels. I'm not a natural TV presenter or a travel guide. I'm not a celebrity chef or wanting to be. I'm just a cook from Melbourne who loves his life and all that it encompasses. My journey has taken me through the ancient lands of Persia, the Ottoman Empire, Phoenicia.

the Moors and the coastal paradise of Andalucía. I have met people who have opened their homes to me and shared their cuisine, history and culture, but above all they have shared with me a piece of their hearts and their lives. I hope I have been able to do justice to the people who have given me so much. I hope I have portrayed their homelands in a manner that they are proud of. And I hope that I have created food that is respectful to the history and love in each special dish or item of produce that they shared.

I hope you enjoy the food and cultures I have visited during my spice journey. The recipes are all rock solid and tasty. A few have already become staples among my family and friends, and I hope the same will happen in your home soon. Cook with this book, use it, dirty it up and put these recipes to the test. Food is something that unites people through a common ground. It is the medium for conversation and gives people a voice irrespective of race, religion, sex or nationality.

Make these recipes your own, add your own words and give it your own accent. People have been doing just that for centuries and that's what makes food special and why I love being a cook.

Saha!
SHANE DELIA

MALTA

Our Lady of Mount Carmel Church, St Julian's Bay

This was where it all started for me as a cook—the home of my ancestors and the place where the penny finally dropped and I decided that I was going to dedicate the rest of my life to hospitality.

T he Delia family motto is *Fortis et Hospitalis,* which means 'strength through hospitality'. I have it tattooed on my arm and the older I get, the more I understand what it really means.

My family's homeland of Malta is a deeply misunderstood little rock. The rest of the world doesn't know what to make of it. Situated in the middle of the Mediterranean Sea, people think we are Italian, though we speak a language that has all the bones of Arabic and 95 per cent of us are Roman Catholic. Over the centuries we have been invaded by nearly everyone wanting a piece of the European pie. And yet we seem to endure.

I grew up in a large Maltese family in Melbourne, Australia. Tales of 'back home' conjured a magical place where the summers were long and hot, adventure was around every corner, and happiness awaited with every plate of food. As much as my dad was 'Australian', he was always Maltese—I mean, it is hard to disguise. Our family has dark skin, Arabic features and, no matter how hard you try, you can never quite shake off that very distinctive Maltese accent. I always wanted to get to know what made my dad the amazing person he was and finally, when I was 14, I was given that chance. Dad decided to take the whole family on a three-month vacation to Malta, to experience firsthand the country he grew up in.

We walked the same streets Dad did as a child, swam in the same waters, cooked and ate the same food with our family and friends, and drank in the same bars he did as a young man. We were thrown into a big, boisterous life that was not really ours, yet we were made to feel like we belonged. I immediately felt a very real connection to my ancestral home. All the stories of my father's youth came rushing in as if they were my own memories—tales from my grandparents about happy times eating and drinking, celebrating festive days by the jewel-blue Mediterranean Sea.

*Malta is a deeply misunderstood little rock. The rest of the world doesn't know what to make of it.*

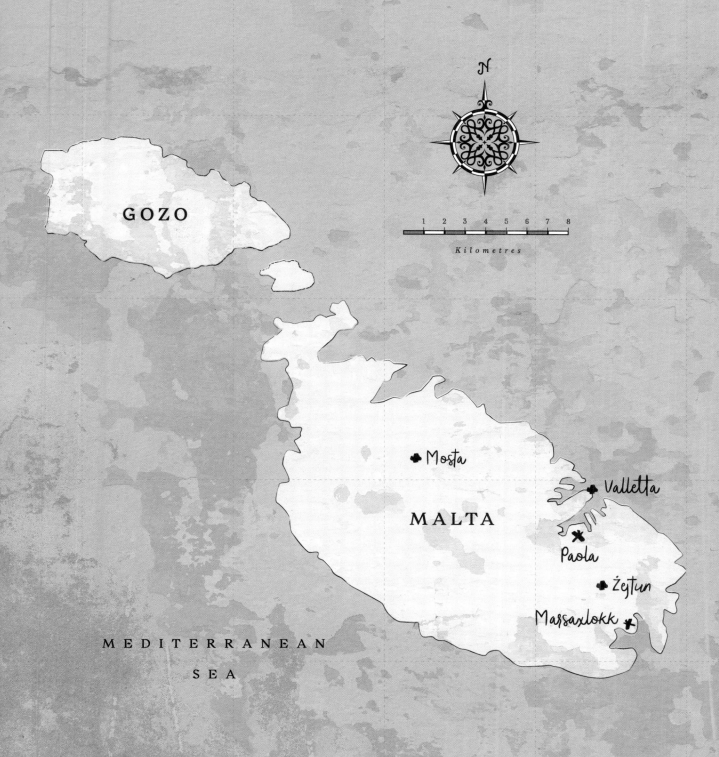

As a kid back in Melbourne I had been under a lot of pressure to choose what I wanted to do with my life. It felt like an impossible decision. I knew that staying in school and pursuing a higher education was not really my calling, but I also knew that I needed something that not only challenged my intellect, but also stirred my soul—something I could connect with other people through. So whether Dad knew it or not, our trip to Malta turned out to be the perfect opportunity to open my mind, my eyes and my heart to what my soul needed.

I was immersed into a slower world: simpler, quieter and clearer. I got the chance to listen to the sounds of day-to-day village life, rather than a busy suburb—to hear people talk and laugh, to watch the elders move about gossiping and berating the young, to stroll the streets taking it all in. And gradually, I realised that it was food that was binding us all together—from the packed lunch we would prepare in the morning to take with us on the long trek to our local limestone beach, to the dinner my family prepared with produce grown or reared by their own hands.

According to Maltese lore, the baker had always been the unofficial village mayor and our family had held that role for generations. Hospitality is in my blood, I realised. It is something I can neither hide nor deny. I was destined to walk the path of my ancestors, but it took coming home to this little island to hear their voice and acknowledge my path.

These days Malta has a very calming effect on me. It can be full of noise, laughter and celebration one minute, and then so quiet the next that you can hear your own heart beat. I love knowing that these ancient towns have seen some amazing things, and feel soothed by my father's hometown, Zejtun. I love the hole-in-the-wall vendors who sell pastizzi and the tiny bars scattered throughout the city that serve an array of little meze to snack on while you sip beautiful Maltese wines or beer; the nannas cooking bagilla and sweet m'quaret in their kitchens, anticipating the next visit of their grandchildren; and the weathered fishermen fixing their nets in the port of Marsaxlokk where every fishing boat has a Phoenician eye painted on its bow. I adore the carob, olives, dates, figs, spices and oranges that fill the terraced fields of Gozo and that are an integral part of our cuisine. All of it linking us back through the ancient Phoenician bloodline that the Maltese people share. ✱

I love the hole-in-the-wall vendors who sell pastizzi and the tiny bars scattered throughout the city that serve an array of little meze.

# PORK AND PEA PASTIZZI WITH MUSTARD MAYONNAISE

I have been eating pastizzi my whole life. To say I love them is a HUGE understatement. But while I may be a chef with Maltese heritage, I have to admit I'm probably the world's worst pastizzi maker, and when I cooked them on my spice journey it was my first proper attempt. What I discovered, though, like with most things, with a little practice and patience, you will get them right.

I'm a simple guy who has always stuck to the classic ricotta filling, but every now and then when I know the spicing is right and I'm in the mood I'll venture over to the other side and snack on a few pea pastizzi. So this recipe is me pushing the boundaries a little with this classic, and I love the way it's turned out. The pork and pea mix has a great taste and texture, and the introduction of the mustard mayo is the bomb!

Pastizzi freeze really well. This recipe makes a large quantity, but as the process is quite fiddly, it's a good idea to make a large batch, so set aside enough time and get some helpers.

### Pork and pea filling

3 star anise

2 cinnamon sticks

10 cloves

2 tablespoons sabaht baharat (Lebanese 7 spice)

3 tablespoons light brown sugar

250 ml (9 fl oz/1 cup) soy sauce

60 ml (2 fl oz/¼ cup) fish sauce

2 small garlic cloves, crushed

1 kg (2 lb 4 oz) pork shoulder

350 g (12 oz) peas, blanched or frozen

1 large handful mint, picked and leaves finely chopped

3 tablespoons dried mint

250 g (9 oz) almonds

### Pastizzi dough

1 kg (2 lb 4 oz) plain (all-purpose) flour, plus extra for dusting

50 g (1 ¾ oz) salt flakes

300 g (10½ oz) butter, at room temperature

### Mustard mayonnaise

300 g (10½ oz) mayonnaise

2 tablespoons dijon mustard

1 tablespoon honey

### PORK AND PEA FILLING

Combine the spices, brown sugar, soy sauce, fish sauce and garlic using a mortar and pestle to make a paste. Rub the pork shoulder with the paste, then cover and place in the fridge overnight.

Preheat the oven to 160°C (315°F/Gas 2–3).

Place the pork in a flameproof casserole dish, cover with water, cover the dish with foil and slowly cook in the oven for 4–6 hours or until the pork is tender and falling apart. Remove the pork from the dish and set aside to cool. Place the dish over high heat, bring the braising liquid to the boil, then reduce the heat to medium and simmer for 20 minutes to make a thick sauce.

When the pork is cool enough to handle, flake the pork and pull it apart. Add to the thickened sauce along with the peas. Finish with the chopped mint, dried mint and almonds.

### PASTIZZI DOUGH

To make the pastizzi dough, using an electric mixer with the dough hook attachment, combine the flour, salt and 750 ml (26 fl oz/3 cups) of water at a moderate speed for 6–8 minutes, until the dough is smooth and comes away cleanly from the side of the bowl. Cover the bowl with a tea towel (dish towel) and leave to rest for 30 minutes.

Alternatively, this dough can be mixed by hand. It will take about 20 minutes.

Sprinkle some flour on your work surface and flatten the dough with a rolling pin until 5 mm (¼ inch) thick, then smear liberally with some of the softened butter. Roll the dough into a log 10 cm (4 inch) thick and then wrap into a coil shape. Cover in plastic wrap and refrigerate for 2 hours or until firm.

Remove the dough from the fridge and allow to soften a little. Cut the coil into quarters. Stretch each piece of dough into a long rectangle. Smear softened butter over the surface of each piece, then roll each piece into a log 10 cm (4 inch) thick, again, then cut into ten portions roughly 2.5 cm (1 inch) thick to make 40 portions.

To make the pastizzi, hold a pastry portion flattened out over your thumb and index finger. Insert a tablespoon of pork and pea filling then, in one swift motion, fold over the filling to encase it, and then flick back the other way and pinch the edges. Repeat this process until the filling and pastry are finished.

Preheat the oven to 200°C (400°F/Gas 6). Line three large baking trays with baking paper.

Place the pastizzi on the prepared trays and cook for 6–8 minutes until the pastizzi are golden.

## MUSTARD MAYONNAISE
Combine the ingredients in a mixing bowl. Cover and refrigerate until required.

## TO SERVE
Serve the pastizzi hot with the mustard mayonnaise.

Note It is a good idea to start this recipe one day ahead.

Pork and pea pastizzi with
mustard mayonnaise

REBECCA.

# RABBIT STEW WITH SULTANA GREMOLATA

For me, no one cooked this dish, called Stuffat tal-fenek in Maltese, better than my nannu Nenu. I grew up with him making me this dish for Sunday lunches at his house. His influence on my life and my cooking has been the foundation I have built my world on. So when I was travelling in Gozo and met Joe at Ta Mena and he said he was going to cook me Fenek, I was a bit worried. No way his version could be better then Nannu's!

To be honest, I wasn't expecting much when I sat down to try the dish, but that's where it all changed. The first mouthful I tasted was amazing—sweet, spice tones, thick sauce and tender juicy rabbit. I was blown away, and I couldn't wipe the smile off my face. But even though it was beautiful, you can't get me to say it was better than Nannu's. I can say, though, that the next time I go to Gozo I'll be knocking on Joe's door and expecting a bowl of that wonderful rabbit stew.

1 whole white farmed rabbit (about 800 g/1 lb 12 oz)
60 ml (2 fl oz/¼ cup) olive oil
2 cinnamon sticks
¼ teaspoon ground cloves
1 teaspoon ground turmeric
½ teaspoon ground cumin
½ teaspoon ground coriander
2 brown onions, diced
3 tablespoons light brown sugar
1 teaspoon salt flakes
1 teaspoon malt vinegar
3 tablespoons tomato paste (concentrated purée)
750 ml (26 fl oz/3 cups) dry red wine

## Sultana gremolata

1 baguette
2 tablespoons ghee (or clarified butter), melted
80 g (2¾ oz/½ cup) pine nuts, toasted
100 g (3½ oz) sultanas (golden raisins)
small handful flat-leaf (Italian) parsley, leaves picked
zest of 2 lemons

Break the rabbit into large chunks or ask your butcher to do this for you. Season with salt and freshly ground black pepper.

Heat 2 tablespoons of the olive oil in a flameproof casserole dish over high heat. Add the rabbit pieces and cook for a few minutes on each side until evenly browned. Remove the meat and set aside. Add the spices, onion, sugar, salt and malt vinegar to the dish and cook for a few minutes until the onion has softened. Add the tomato paste and stir through, then return the rabbit to the dish, add the wine and cook for about 15 minutes until the sauce has thickened.

Add enough water to cover the rabbit, place a lid on top, and simmer for about 1½ hours or until the meat comes away from the bone. Remove the rabbit from the dish, gently pull the meat away from the bones and discard the bones.

Meanwhile, preheat the oven to 180°C (350°F/Gas 4).

To make the sultana gremolata, put the baguette in a food processor and blend into a coarse crumb. Transfer the crumb onto a baking tray and pour over the ghee, coating evenly. Cook for 8 minutes or until golden brown. Remove from the oven and, while still hot, mix through the pine nuts, sultanas, parsley and lemon zest.

Divide the rabbit between six serving bowls and top with the sauce. Drizzle over the remaining oil, sprinkle over the sultana gremolata and serve.

The fishing port, Marsaxlokk

Mohammad Al-Amin Mosque, Beirut

# LEBANON

**I thought I was prepared for what Lebanon was going to show me, but once I became immersed I quickly realised that this place was going to be so much more then I'd ever imagined.**

Lebanon is special to me for more than just food. Maha, my wife, is of Lebanese descent, and the region is also the place where my Phoenician ancestors set sail into the Mediterranean, taking food, wine and art to the rest of the world.

The food culture of Lebanon is about more than just a meal—it is part of the national identity, a reason for living. When winter draws to an end, so comes the most important season in the Lebanese cookbook ... Spring brings new life and the country celebrates its diverse regional crops. The rush is on to capture its beauty and freshness, to harvest those flavours for the months ahead. Fruit is preserved, orange blossoms and rose petals distilled, herbs and spices dried, vegetables pickled, wheat and yoghurt fermented, and spring lamb is slow cooked in its own fat. All of which create the intricate and diverse base to Lebanon's cuisine.

But what really took me by surprise on my spice journey to Lebanon and put a huge smile on my face was the overwhelming hospitality of the people and their live-for-today mentality. People opened their homes and welcomed me as family. Their generosity of spirit to give without expectation touched me deeply, and the pride and happiness I witnessed when people shared secret family recipes was truly overwhelming.

Beirut itself is like no other city I have ever been to. One moment you are walking past an ancient monument, almost inhaling its presence and imagining what things would have been like thousands of years ago when Lebanon was a magical place, the next you look to your left and see the shelled-out buildings that serve as a constant reminder of the stress and uncertainty that colours the recent past.

Lebanon is a contradiction on so many levels, but it all adds to the charm and beauty of the place. It has a sturdy soul that seems capable of getting through anything and is ever-present no matter where you go. From the snow-capped mountains, through the produce-rich Bekaa Valley, along the sun-kissed coast, to the rock-star-studded beauty of the Corniche promenade in Beirut—Lebanon excites me and has drawn me in. ✶

*The food culture of Lebanon is about more than just a meal— it is a part of the national identity, a reason for living.*

Preparation time: 20 minutes plus 5 hours curing • Cooking time: nil • Serves: 6

# ARAK-CURED KINGFISH WITH SMASHED RADISH DRESSING

**I was so amazed with the quality and the variety of the seafood on offer in Lebanon—so fresh—and the atmosphere in the Tripoli fish markets really got my heart pumping. This dish pays tribute to the fresh vibrant seafood that is one of the real hidden gems of Lebanon.**

### Arak-cured kingfish

- 250 g (9 oz) rock salt
- 250 g (9 oz) caster (superfine) sugar
- 5 star anise
- 10 za'atar* sprigs (or thyme sprigs)
- 120 ml (3¾ fl oz) Lebanese arak (or ouzo or Pernod)
- small handful thyme
- 1 side sashimi-grade kingfish (about 1.5 kg/3 lb 5 oz), skin removed

### Smashed radish dressing

- 1 preserved lemon, peel only, finely diced
- 2 French shallots, finely diced
- 1 teaspoon black Aleppo pepper* (pul biber)
- 1 tablespoon orange blossom water*
- 2½ tablespoons olive oil
- 6 French breakfast radishes (or other radishes)

- 60 g (2¼ oz/¼ cup) Kewpie mayonnaise, to serve
- rocket (arugula) leaves, to serve (optional)

Mix all the kingfish curing ingredients together in a bowl.

Place the kingfish on a tray and cover with the curing mixture. Cover with plastic wrap and refrigerate for 5 hours to cure (see note).

Meanwhile, to make the smashed radish dressing, mix all the ingredients, except the radishes, together in a bowl. Smash the radishes with the underside of a heavy-based saucepan. Add the radishes to the bowl and toss through to coat.

Shake off the salt mixture from the kingfish and rinse off any excess. Pat dry with paper towel and then slice into 5 mm (¼ inch) slices.

Arrange the sliced kingfish on each serving plate. Add small dollops of mayonnaise, top with radish, spoon over any remaining dressing, scatter over the rocket, if using, and serve.

**Note** It is important to remove the fish from the cure after 5 hours to stop the curing process.

# GRILLED HALOUMI WITH POMEGRANATE AND SUMAC DRESSING

Simplicity and freshness, for me, are the two things any good cuisine is built on.

This dish is one you see all throughout Lebanon. I remember driving from Beirut to Sidon and stopping on the side of the road at a simple store where a man with a huge moustache was making fresh cheese sandwiches—one man, a toaster, some labneh, haloumi, a mound of fresh flat bread, spices, olive oil and a few other bits and pieces. He had a line out the door!

This man cooked me a toasted sandwich with haloumi and za'atar drizzled with olive oil and local sea salt. I sat on the kerb out the front of his shop and savoured every mouthful. Simple, fresh and cooked with love. Heaven.

Combine all the ingredients, except the haloumi, in a mixing bowl. Check for seasoning and adjust if necessary.

Heat a large chargrill pan or frying pan over high heat. Add the haloumi and cook for 1 minute on each side or until golden. Press the haloumi with a spatula; when there is no resistance the haloumi is cooked. Remove the haloumi from the pan and transfer onto paper towel to drain, then divide among serving plates. Drizzle over the pomegranate and sumac dressing and serve immediately.

1 teaspoon pepitas (pumpkin seeds), toasted
seeds from 1 small pomegranate
1 tablespoon pomegranate molasses*
1 teaspoon za'atar* (or dried thyme)
1 cocktail onion, finely diced
1 teaspoon pine nuts, toasted
1 tablespoon sumac*
a few rosemary sprigs
150 ml (5½ fl oz) olive oil
pinch of salt flakes
300 g (10½ oz) haloumi cheese, sliced into 1 cm (½ inch) thick portions

Preparation time: 10 minutes • Cooking time: 35 minutes • Serves: 4

# SHELLFISH MOGHRABIEH

**Tripoli is one of those places that has little secrets around every corner. I found so many beautiful dishes while visiting there—fish, sweets, killer hummus—and in the winding alleys of the ancient souk I stumbled across traditional handmade moghrabieh (Lebanese couscous).**

**A great technique I picked up is to boil a whole peeled onion in a saucepan of water to soften it, then dice it and fold it through the fresh cinnamon-spiced pearl couscous. It gives the onion a really soft and sweet texture, but still keeps it crisp and sharp—a real surprise and point of difference in such a simple street-food dish.**

- 1 brown onion, peeled
- 350 g (12 oz) pearl couscous (moghrabieh)
- 1 tablespoon olive oil
- 1 tablespoon butter
- 12 raw prawns (shrimp), peeled and deveined, tails left intact
- 12 scallops
- 120 g (4¼ oz) tinned chickpeas, rinsed and drained
- 2 tablespoons ground cinnamon
- handful chopped thyme
- 2 tablespoons lemon juice
- 2 French breakfast radishes (or other radishes), thinly shaved
- 2 baby turnips, thinly shaved
- small handful mint leaves, to serve

Cook the onion in a saucepan of lightly salted boiling water over medium–high heat for 15 minutes, then remove with a slotted spoon and set aside to cool. Add the pearl couscous to the pan and cook for 10–12 minutes or until softened. Drain and set aside. Chop the onion.

Heat the olive oil and butter in a frying pan over high heat, then add the prawns and scallops and cook for a few minutes, until just opaque. Add the pearl couscous to the pan, along with the chopped onion, chickpeas, cinnamon and thyme. Toss to combine, then cook for 2 minutes to warm through. Remove from the heat, add the lemon juice and season with salt.

Place the shellfish moghrabieh into bowls and scatter over the shaved vegetables and mint. Serve immediately.

# CRACKED WHEAT AND TOMATO KIBBEH

**Talk about my idea of heaven ... Sitting on the beach with my feet in the sand listening to the sounds of Lebanese pop music drifting through the air, watching children play in the water, an ice-cold Lebanese beer in one hand and eating simply cooked line-caught fish with this beautiful vegetarian tomato kibbeh. I don't know how you could top it.**

Soak the burghul in a bowl of hot tap water for 30 minutes or until soft. Drain.

Grind the burghul, tomato and onion using a food processor, into an even consistency. Alternatively, use a mincer. Transfer the burghul mixture into a bowl and add the remaining ingredients, tasting as you go to balance the flavours. Adjust, if one flavour dominates, by adding more of the other ingredients. Cover with plastic wrap and refrigerate until required.

Place the radish, beetroot, onion and rocket into separate bowls of iced water and leave to crisp for about 10 minutes. Drain on paper towel.

Put the burghul mixture onto a serving plate and add a few dollops of yoghurt. Top with the thinly sliced vegetables, rocket and tomatoes. Drizzle with olive oil and serve immediately.

## Kibbeh

265 g (9¼ oz/1½ cups) fine burghul (bulgur)
1 large tomato
½ red onion
1 tablespoon dried mint
1 tablespoon sumac*
1 teaspoon smoked paprika
pinch of cayenne pepper
1 tablespoon capsicum paste*
2 tablespoons pomegranate molasses*
10 mint leaves, finely chopped
10 coriander (cilantro) leaves, finely chopped
drizzle of olive oil

1 radish, thinly sliced
1 candy beetroot (beet) (or another heirloom beetroot), thinly sliced
1 cocktail onion, thinly sliced
handful rocket (arugula) leaves
handful small heirloom tomatoes, halved
50 g (1¾ oz) Greek-style yoghurt
drizzle of extra virgin olive oil

The coast near Anfeh

# LAMB AND KISHK KIBBEH

I am mad about sour flavours and in today's cooking we in the West all seem to be getting excited about preservation and fermentation in food.

I remember watching women lying out freshly made kishk paste on muslin on a rooftop in the Lebanese foothills so it could ferment and dry under the warm Lebanese sun—in the Middle East this kind of stuff has been going on since time began.

To make the casing, soak the burghul in a bowl of hot tap water for 30 minutes or until soft. Drain well, as you don't want excess moisture in this casing.

Tip the burghul into a food processor and add the sabaht baharat, salt and lamb, and combine well. Transfer into a bowl, cover with plastic wrap and refrigerate until required.

To make the kishk farce, bring a saucepan of water to the boil over medium–high heat. Score the bases of the tomatoes, then blanch them for 10 seconds. Refresh the tomatoes in iced water, then peel off the skins and discard. Quarter the tomatoes, remove the seeds and cut them into 1 cm (½ inch) dice.

Combine the tomatoes and remaining ingredients in a bowl, and mix together to a sticky consistency. Season to taste.

To make the kibbeh, put an egg-sized amount of the casing mixture in your hand and form it into a ball. Poke a hole in the ball with your finger and then make a space for the filling with a tablespoon. Add a teaspoon of the filling and pinch the top to seal the ball. Repeat with the remaining casing and filling mixtures to make about 30 kibbeh.

Pour some canola oil into a deep frying pan, about 4 cm (1½ inches) deep, then heat over medium–high heat until it shimmers. If you have a kitchen thermometer, the oil will be ready when the temperature reaches 180°C (350°F). Alternatively, use a deep-fryer.

Carefully add the kibbeh to the pan in batches and cook for 3–5 minutes or until golden brown. Drain on paper towel, then serve with some yoghurt.

**Note** Kishk powder is made from fermented burghul and yoghurt, which is then dried and ground into a powder. It is available at specialist Middle Eastern grocery shops and online.

300 g (10½ oz) fine burghul (bulgur)
1 teaspoon sabaht baharat*
    (Lebanese 7 spice)
360 g (12¾ oz) lean minced (ground)
    lamb leg
pinch of salt flakes
canola oil, for deep-frying

### Kishk farce filling
4 oxheart tomatoes
½ brown onion, finely diced
4 silverbeet (Swiss chard) stalks,
    leaves finely chopped
160 g (5½ oz) tinned chickpeas,
    rinsed, drained and smashed
100 g (3½ oz) kishk powder
    (see note)
50 g (1¾ oz) Greek-style yoghurt,
    plus extra to serve
2 tablespoons dried mint
drizzle of olive oil

# STUFFED CHICKEN WINGS WITH SOUR CHERRY BARBECUE SAUCE

**Street food in Beirut is a big deal. Hundreds of hole-in-the-wall vendors and street-side food sellers all produce killer, cheap bites that are hard to beat. This is a dish that pays homage to the Armenian community in Beirut who cook skilfully flavoured street-food dishes using sweet and sour tones, all balanced out with heat and spice.**

Remove the casings from the sucuk sausages. Fill the cavities of the chicken wings with about 1 tablespoon of the sucuk mince.

Bring a saucepan of water to the boil over medium–high heat. Place half the chicken wings in a bamboo steamer with at least 1 cm (½ inch) gap between them and place the steamer on top of the pan. Steam for 10–15 minutes—the steaming process will cause the cooked chicken meat to plump up a little. To check if they are cooked properly, you can use a skewer. Push the skewer through the middle and leave for 10 seconds, when it comes out, it should feel 'blood temperature', not cold on the fingertips. Transfer the stuffed chicken wings onto a plate and repeat with the remaining stuffed chicken wings. Cover the plate with plastic wrap and refrigerate until fully cold.

Combine the plain flour, garlic powder, onion powder, sweet paprika, cayenne pepper, salt, black pepper, tomato soup powder, rice flour and cornflakes in a large bowl. Mix evenly. Set aside until required.

To make the sour cherry barbecue sauce, combine the remaining ingredients, except the puréed sour cherries, with 250 ml (9 fl oz/1 cup) of water in a saucepan over medium–high heat. Bring to the boil, then reduce to a simmer and cook, uncovered, stirring frequently, for 40 minutes. Remove the saucepan from the heat and add the puréed sour cherries. Set aside to cool.

Put the buttermilk in a bowl. Remove the chicken wings from the fridge and place, one at a time, in the buttermilk to lightly coat.

Transfer into the flour mixture and roll around to evenly coat. Transfer onto a tray and repeat the process until all the chicken wings are crumbed.

Pour some canola oil into a deep frying pan, about 4 cm (1½ inches) deep, then heat over medium–high heat until it shimmers. If you have a kitchen thermometer, the oil will be ready when the temperature reaches 180°C (350°F). Alternatively, use a deep-fryer. Carefully add the chicken wings to the pan, a few at a time, and deep fry for 3–4 minutes, until golden brown. Drain on paper towel.

Serve immediately with the sour cherry barbecue sauce.

500 g (1 lb 2 oz) sucuk sausages*
16 boneless chicken wings (mid section only—about 60 g/2¼ oz each)
500 g (1 lb 2 oz/3⅓ cup) plain (all-purpose) flour
2½ tablespoons garlic powder
2½ tablespoons onion powder
1½ tablespoons sweet paprika
1½ tablespoons cayenne pepper
2 tablespoons salt flakes
1 teaspoon freshly ground black pepper
80 g (2¾ oz) instant tomato soup powder
100 g (3½ oz) rice flour
100 g (3½ oz/3⅓ cup) cornflakes, coarsely crushed
600 ml (21 fl oz) buttermilk
canola oil, for deep-frying

**Sour cherry barbecue sauce**

500 ml (17 fl oz/2 cups) tomato sauce (ketchup)
250 ml (9 fl oz/1 cup) apple cider vinegar
70 g (2½ oz) light brown sugar
70 g (2½ oz) sugar
2 teaspoons freshly ground black pepper
2 teaspoons onion powder
2 teaspoons mustard powder
1 tablespoon lemon juice
1 tablespoon worcestershire sauce
400 ml (14 fl oz) sour cherry juice
300 g (10½ oz) pitted sour cherries, puréed

# SPICY DAHLIA CHIPS

Every now and then on my spice journey I meet people who really leave their mark on me. It's not always their cooking skills that stay with me, sometimes it can just be a personal connection. This was the case with a young woman who was punching above her weight in a male-dominated culture and industry. Dahlia ran a little pop up fish restaurant right on the beach in the town of Tyre, called Cloud 59. Her power, confidence, attitude and swagger made me smile.

Give these chips a try. The recipe uses frozen chips as a starting point, so it is super simple, and the use of chilli and spices really ramps up an old classic. I guarantee the hardest part will be stopping yourself from making a second batch straight away. Thanks Dahlia!

Pour some canola oil into a deep frying pan, about 4 cm (1½ inches) deep, then heat over medium–high heat until it shimmers. If you have a kitchen thermometer, the oil will be ready when the temperature reaches 180°C (350°F). Alternatively, use a deep-fryer. Carefully add the French fries to the pan and cook for 3–5 minutes until golden brown.

Meanwhile, heat the butter in a small saucepan over medium heat for 5 minutes or until nut brown in colour and frothy. Remove from the heat and set aside.

Heat the olive oil in a large frying pan over medium–high heat, add the garlic and sauté until soft and fragrant. Add the chips, straight from the pan, then add the almonds, Aleppo pepper, sumac and ground coriander. Toss really well to ensure all the seasonings are well dispersed. Drizzle over the brown butter and scatter over the coriander leaves. Place in a serving dish with lemon wedges on the side and serve immediately.

**Note** Spicy dahlia chips are great served on their own, but are also delicious served with grilled fish and at barbecues.

canola oil, for deep-frying
500 g (1 lb 2 oz) frozen crinkle-cut French fries
100 g (3½ oz) butter
2 tablespoons olive oil
2 garlic cloves, crushed
50 g (1¾ oz/½ cup) flaked almonds, toasted
pinch of red Aleppo pepper* (pul biber)
pinch of sumac*
pinch of ground coriander
coriander (cilantro) leaves, to serve
lemon wedges, to serve

# DUCK AWARMA

Awarma is not only a really tasty ingredient, but it is a way for people to preserve meat for years on end with no refrigeration. I wanted to take this same technique and introduce a little more spice, using duck instead of the traditional lamb, and I'm really happy with the result.

Once you have this on hand, you can serve it with hummus and flat breads (see page 53), stirred through risotto (see page 54) or as part of a Middle Eastern banquet.

Place the duck in a bowl and completely cover with the salt. Leave to rest for 30 minutes, then rinse off and pat dry with paper towel.

Heat a heavy-based saucepan over high heat. Add the duck meat and cook, stirring frequently, for about 15 minutes until the fat has rendered down and the meat is caramelised. Add the spices and caramelise for another couple of minutes. Reduce the heat to very low, add the duck fat and cook for at least 2 hours. Remove from the heat, transfer into a large sterilised jar and store in the pantry for 2 weeks before use (see note).

**Notes** Duck fat is available from select supermarkets and poultry suppliers. Look for jars or tins. Like other fats, it is solid at room temperature, but melts quickly with heat.

Add additional spices to the preserving jar, if you like, such as star anise, cloves and black peppercorns.

The duck awarma can be stored for at least 3 months.

2 x 180 g (6½ oz) duck breasts, skin and sinews removed, diced
500 g (1 lb 2 oz) rock salt
3 tablespoons sabaht baharat* (Lebanese 7 spice)
4 cardamom pods
2 bay leaves
2 cinnamon sticks
500 g (1 lb 2 oz) duck fat (see note)

# HUMMUS WITH DUCK AWARMA AND CUMIN FLAT BREADS

I loved the time I got to spend with the Druze community in Lebanon, learning their food history—awarma is one of their traditional preserving techniques. This dish combines the sweet notes of duck awarma with the creaminess of hummus, and is served with freshly made cumin flat bread to mop it all up and make a delicious feast of flavour.

## HUMMUS

Put the chickpeas in a food processor and blend until smooth—you may need to frequently scrape down the side to begin with. Add the remaining ingredients and 200 ml (7 fl oz) of hot tap water and blend to a smooth purée. Taste and adjust the seasoning if necessary. Refrigerate until required.

## CUMIN FLAT BREAD

Using an electric stand mixer with the dough hook attachment, combine the flour, salt, yoghurt, cumin seeds, garlic and 130 ml (4 fl oz) of lukewarm water at a moderate speed for 5–7 minutes, until the dough is smooth and comes away cleanly from the side of the bowl. Be careful not to overwork as it becomes tough. Cover the bowl with a tea towel (dish towel) and leave the dough to rest in a warm place for 30 minutes to double in size. Divide into six, roll into balls and allow to prove again on a baking tray, covered, for about 20 minutes.

Sprinkle some flour on your work surface and flatten the dough with a rolling pin until 2 mm (1/16 inch) thick. Leave to prove for 10 minutes.

Heat a frying pan or grill pan over high heat. Lightly brush with olive oil and then add the flat breads, one at a time, and cook for about 2 minutes on each side until crisp and browned. Keep warm.

## TO ASSEMBLE

Heat a frying pan over high heat. Add the duck awarma and the nuts. Cook for 4–5 minutes, stirring frequently to allow the nuts to evenly colour and the duck to warm through. Add the baby figs, cook for another 30 seconds and stir through until well combined.

Spoon the hummus into the centre of a serving dish, make a well in the middle and pour in the duck mixture. Place the cumin flat breads on the side and serve immediately.

### Hummus

300 g (10½ oz) tinned chickpeas, rinsed and drained
100 g (3½ oz) tahini*
2 garlic cloves
150 ml (5 fl oz) lemon juice
2 tablespoons salt flakes
50 ml (1½ fl oz) olive oil

### Cumin flat bread

300 g (10½ oz/2 cups) plain (all-purpose) flour, plus extra for dusting
1 teaspoon salt flakes
40 g (1½ oz) Greek-style yoghurt
1 teaspoon toasted and coarsely crushed cumin seeds
2 garlic cloves, pounded using a mortar and pestle
olive oil, for frying

### To assemble

1 quantity duck awarma (see page 50)
50 g (1¾ oz/¼ cup) pine nuts
50 g (1¾ oz) blanched almonds
150 g (5½ oz) dried baby figs, soaked (or fresh figs when in season)

# FREEKEH RISOTTO WITH DUCK AWARMA, POACHED EGGS AND TOASTED NUTS

This is the one dish in Lebanon that I can honestly say really took my breath away. Simple but complex flavour all brought together by that amazing grain, freekeh. So beautiful.

The Bekaa Valley is the food centre of Lebanon—its nutrient-rich soil gives life to everything that it produces. So when I had the chance to drink wine from the ancient Phoenician region that gave birth to all viticulture around the world and eat this simple humble dish sourced from local fields, how could I say no?

Soak the freekeh in a bowl of water overnight. Drain.

Bring the chicken stock to the boil in a saucepan over medium–high heat.

Heat the olive oil in a frying pan over medium–low heat, add the onions and cook for about 5 minutes to caramelise. Add the wine and allow to reduce by half, then add the drained freekeh and stir through. Add a ladleful of stock and stir through until it has been absorbed, then continue to cook, adding the stock, a ladleful at a time, for 25–30 minutes until all the stock has been added and the freekeh has the appearance of a risotto.

Meanwhile, place a wide-based saucepan over high heat, add the duck awarma and some of the duck fat from the jar, the nuts, cinnamon, bay leaf and sabaht baharat, and gently cook until golden. Remove from the heat and set aside.

Sprinkle the chopped herbs and rocket into the risotto, fold through the butter, season, and divide between each serving dish. Spoon the duck and nut mixture on top. Using the back of a spoon, make divots for the eggs to be placed in. Carefully add the eggs—being careful not to pop the yolk—and then grate some kefalograviera over the top. Serve immediately.

200 g (7 oz) freekeh
1 litre (35 fl oz/4 cups) chicken stock
2 tablespoons olive oil
2 onions, finely diced
250 ml (9 fl oz/1 cup) dry white wine
3 tablespoons duck awarma
  (see page 50)
100 g (3½ oz) walnuts, halved
50 g (1¾ oz/⅓ cup) pine nuts
100 g (3½ oz) blanched almonds
1 cinnamon stick
1 bay leaf
1 teaspoon sabaht baharat*
  (Lebanese 7 spice)
2 handfuls flat-leaf (Italian) parsley,
  finely chopped
2 handfuls coriander (cilantro),
  leaves finely chopped
handful rocket (arugula) leaves
50 g (1¾ oz) butter, diced small
4 soft-poached eggs, to serve
100 g (3½ oz) kefalograviera cheese
  (or another hard sheep's cheese)

# LAMB SFIHA

You can really tell a lot about a country by the quality of its street food. And if Lebanon was going to be judged this way, then these little parcels of heaven from Baalbek would get my vote!

So simple, but soooo tasty, these little mini pizzas are the type of food I really love. Great dough, really fresh ingredients and when they are cooked right in front of you and you can sit on the side of the road and eat them— well, that's what life is all about.

Put the lamb, pumpkin, onion, garlic, Aleppo peppers and tomatoes in a food processor and mix until well combined. Season with salt and pepper. Keep refrigerated until required.

Dissolve the yeast in 400 ml (14 fl oz) of water in a bowl.

Combine the flour and salt in an electric stand mixer bowl and attach the hook attachment. Commence mixing on a low speed and slowly add the yeast and water mixture, and the olive oil. Increase the speed slightly and mix for 5–8 minutes until smooth.

Sprinkle some flour on a tray. Divide the dough into 20 balls and place on the tray. Cover with a tea towel (dish towel) and set aside in a warm place for 20–30 minutes to double in size.

Preheat the oven to 200°C (400°F/Gas 6).

Sprinkle some flour on your work surface and, using a rolling pin, flatten the dough balls into a square shape about 3 mm (⅛ inch) thick. Place a tablespoon of the lamb mixture in the middle of a square and flatten it out. Pinch together two opposite corners and repeat with the other side. You should end up with four-pinched cornered pastry squares with the filling in the middle. Repeat until you have used all the mixture and dough.

Place the sfiha on a preheated pizza stone or baking tray and cook for about 3–5 minutes until golden. Remove from the oven, scatter over the mint leaves and serve with lemon cheeks.

800 g (1 lb 12 oz) lean minced (ground) lamb leg
200 g (7 oz) jap or kent pumpkin (winter squash), roughly chopped
1 red onion, roughly chopped
2 garlic cloves, roughly chopped
1 tablespoon red Aleppo pepper* (pul biber)
1 tablespoon black Aleppo pepper* (pul biber)
2 vine-ripened tomatoes, roughly chopped
20 g (¾ oz) dried yeast
625 g (1 lb 6 oz) strong flour, plus extra for dusting
2 teaspoons salt flakes
splash of olive oil
handful mint, leaves picked
lemon cheeks, to serve

# RICOTTA AND CAROB LADY FINGERS

Carob is one of those ingredients that people don't really understand or don't give too much respect to. I have to admit I used to be one of those people, too, but after travelling through Malta and Lebanon I started to realise how beautiful carob is and how important it once was. Did you know, so the story goes, that carob seeds were originally used as the standard measure for precious stones? Over time the word corrupted, and we now have the word 'carat'.

Line a large bowl with muslin (cheesecloth). Place the ricotta in the muslin and leave to drain, covered, in the fridge overnight.

Combine the drained ricotta, carob and almonds in a bowl and stir well.

Place 2 tablespoons of the ricotta filling onto a piece of brik pastry and roll into a log shape, then fold in the edges. Brush the edges with the egg yolk to seal. Repeat this process until all the pastry is used, to make about 8 fingers.

Pour some canola oil into a frying pan, about 4 cm (1½ inches) deep, then heat over medium–high heat until it shimmers. If you have a kitchen thermometer, the oil will be ready when the temperature reaches 170°C (325°F). Alternatively, use a deep-fryer. Carefully add the pastries, a few at a time, and deep-fry for 3–4 minutes or until golden brown. Transfer onto paper towel to drain, and dust with icing sugar.

Place the lady fingers on a wooden board or serving platter, garnish with some chocolate fairy floss and serve immediately.

**Notes** This dish is traditionally made with areesh (a drained Lebanese yoghurt), but ricotta is an easy replacement.

You can find carob molasses and chocolate fairy floss at Middle Eastern grocery stores.

200 g (7 oz) ricotta (see note)
115 g (4 oz/⅓ cup) carob molasses (see note)
2 tablespoons flaked almonds, toasted
8 sheets brik pastry*
1 egg yolk
canola oil, for deep-frying
icing (confectioners') sugar, for dusting
80 g (2¾ oz) chocolate fairy floss (pashmak) (see note)

Preparation time: 15 minutes plus 24 hours marinating • Cooking time: 15 minutes • Makes: about 1 kg (2 lb 4 oz)

# CANDIED SPICED PUMPKIN

**The preservation of fruit in the mountains of Lebanon is a celebration of life. Lebanon moves with the seasons and when fruit and vegetables are harvested it's about enjoying them at their peak as well as preserving them for the colder months ahead.**

**I was really touched and inspired by the amazing women I met at Mymoune, an artisan food company and women's refuge in the Lebanese foothills. Their story, passion and skill really resonated with me, and opened my world to some wonderful creations.**

**I love this recipe because it shows the beauty of pumpkin—such a simple vegetable often overlooked as just a soup vegetable or a side to be served with a Sunday roast.**

- 600 g (1 lb 5 oz) sugar
- 10 cloves
- 12 cardamom pods, crushed
- 2 vanilla beans, split and seeds scraped
- 1 bay leaf
- 1 cinnamon stick
- 1 kg (2 lb 4 oz) jap or kent pumpkin (winter squash)
- 100 ml (3½ fl oz) orange blossom water*

Place the sugar, cloves, cardamom pods, vanilla beans and seeds, bay leaf, cinnamon stick and 600 ml (21 fl oz) of water in a large saucepan and bring to the boil over high heat. Reduce the heat and simmer for 5 minutes or until the sugar has dissolved. Set aside.

Cut the pumpkin in half and scrape out the seeds. Cut into thick wedges.

Bring a large saucepan of water to the boil over high heat. Add the pumpkin, reduce the heat to a simmer and cook for 10 minutes or until the pumpkin is soft but still holding its shape. Carefully remove the pumpkin from the pan and divide between sterilised jars. Add the orange blossom water and the spiced syrup to the jars to cover the pumpkin, cover with lids and then refrigerate for at least 24 hours so the pumpkin takes on the flavour of the syrup.

**Notes** Kept in the fridge, candied spiced pumpkin will keep for at least 3 months.

Serve as an accompaniment with the fig and walnut ice cream (see page 62). Use as the basis for pumpkin Turkish delight (see page 161).

# FIG AND WALNUT ICE CREAM

These flavours are the soul of the Lebanese mountains. In season, you can smell the sweet toffee aroma oozing out of the sun-ripened figs. Roasted walnuts add a special earthy contrast to the sweet honey-like goodness of the figs in this ice cream. I love this recipe and it's a great one to just sit in front of the TV with, grab a spoon and devour. You don't need an ice cream maker to pull this one off.

To make the fig paste, put the figs and sugar in a saucepan with 500 ml (17 fl oz/ 2 cups) of water over medium heat and stir until the sugar has dissolved. Bring to the boil, then reduce the heat and simmer for 30 minutes or until the figs are really soft. Place the fig mixture in a food processor and purée to make a smooth paste.

Place the caster sugar and 250 ml (9 fl oz/1 cup) of water in a saucepan over low heat and stir to dissolve. Add the fig paste, remove from the heat and use a hand-held stick blender to purée until smooth. Set aside to cool.

Fold the walnuts through the fig mixture.

Beat the egg yolks using an electric stand mixer with the whisk attachment at medium–high speed until thick and pale. Add to the cooled fig paste mix.

Whip the cream to soft peaks using the electric stand mixer with the whisk attachment.

Fold the egg and fig paste mixture into the cream. Pour into a container and freeze for 2–3 hours.

Remove the fig and walnut ice cream from the freezer and leave to soften slightly. Serve with fresh figs and walnuts or with candied spiced pumpkin (see page 61).

## Fig paste

500 g (1 lb 2 oz) dried white figs
440 g (15½ oz/2 cups) sugar

175 g (6 oz) caster (superfine) sugar
200 g (7 oz) walnuts, crushed, plus extra to serve
4 egg yolks
500 ml (17 fl oz/2 cups) thickened (whipping) cream
4 fresh ripe figs, to serve

# ROAST PEANUT BUTTER PARFAIT, TAHINI SALTED CARAMEL AND BROKEN BAKLAVA

Helleb's Sweets in Tripoli is one of the most amazing sweet shops I have ever visited. Entrenched in history and using breathtaking techniques, they produce some stellar, traditional Lebanese sweets. The baklava I tried there was just incredible.

For me a good baklava has to have crunch, a toasted buttery nutty flavour and hints of caramel, normally brought together by the over-the-top sweet syrup it is drenched in. I don't think you can beat the original baklava I tried at Helleb's, so I am not even going to try. This dish pays homage to all the things I love about baklava, but with a twist. It's a great dish that you can cook for friends and family, and claim it as your own. It's a winner!

## ROAST PEANUT BUTTER PARFAIT

Preheat the oven to 170°C (325°F/Gas 3).

Put the peanuts on a baking tray and roast for 8 minutes or until golden brown. Transfer into a food processor and blend until as smooth as possible. Add 300 ml (10½ fl oz) of the cream and continue to blend to a thick peanut butter-like consistency. Set aside.

Whip 325 ml (11 fl oz) of the cream to stiff peaks using an electric stand mixer with the whisk attachment and then set aside.

Combine the peanut mixture with the remaining 75 ml (2¼ fl oz) of cream in a bowl. Fold through the whipped cream. Set aside.

Place the egg yolks in the bowl of the electric mixer and whisk on high speed until pale. Reduce the speed to low and continue to whisk while you make the syrup.

Put the sugar, glucose and 2½ tablespoons of water in a small saucepan over high heat, bring to the boil and cook to soft ball stage—to test if the syrup is ready drop a small amount into a shallow bowl of cold water to cool it down. It should form a soft ball. If you have a kitchen thermometer, the syrup will be ready when the temperature reaches 115–118°C (about 240°F).

Gradually pour the syrup into the egg yolks. Once all the syrup has been added, increase the speed and whip for 15 minutes or until cool.

Fold the egg mixture through the peanut butter cream until well combined. Pour into six serving bowls and freeze for 4 hours.

### Roast peanut butter parfait

200 g (7 oz) peanuts
700 ml (24 fl oz) thickened (whipping) cream
8 egg yolks
250 g (9 oz) caster (superfine) sugar
50 g (1¾ oz) liquid glucose*

### Broken baklava

12 sheets filo pastry, at room temperature
200 g (7 oz) ghee (or clarified butter), melted
100 g (3½ oz/⅔ cup) pine nuts, coarsely crushed
50 g (1¾ oz) walnuts, coarsely crushed
100 g (3½ oz) blanched almonds, coarsely crushed
80 g (2¾ oz) cinnamon sugar (see note)

### Tahini salted caramel

75 g (2½ oz) liquid glucose*
75 g (2½ oz) sugar
75 ml (2¼ fl oz) milk
60 g (2¼ oz) butter
160 ml (5¼ fl oz) thickened (whipping) cream
150 g (5½ oz) tahini*
pinch of salt flakes

### To serve

good quality chocolate ice cream

## BROKEN BAKLAVA

Lay 1 filo sheet on a baking tray and brush with a little ghee. Add a sprinkle of each of the nuts and the cinnamon sugar and then place another layer of filo on top. Brush with more ghee. Continue layering with nuts, cinnamon sugar and filo until all the filo sheets are used, ending up with a layer of filo. Transfer to the fridge and leave for 20 minutes until it sets.

Preheat the oven to 175°C (345°F/Gas 3). Remove the pastry from the fridge.

Put the baklava in the oven and cook for 12 minutes or until golden. Remove from the oven, leave to cool, then break up into shards. Set aside (see note).

## TAHINI SALTED CARAMEL

Combine the glucose, sugar, milk and butter in a saucepan and simmer over medium heat for 5–10 minutes, stirring occasionally, until the mixture thickens and turns creamy caramel in colour.

Meanwhile, put the cream in a separate saucepan and bring to a gentle simmer over low heat.

When the caramel is golden and has thickened add the heated cream, tahini and salt to the pan, and stir through. Pass the mixture through a fine sieve into a bowl to remove any lumps. Set aside.

## TO SERVE

Remove the roast peanut butter parfait and chocolate ice cream from the freezer and set aside to soften slightly.

Place some tahini salted caramel on top of the peanut butter parfait. Top with a scoop of chocolate ice cream, add the broken baklava, and serve.

**Notes** You can buy cinnamon sugar at the supermarket. You can make it, too, combining equal parts ground cinnamon to sugar.

You can make the broken baklava ahead and store in an airtight container.

Roast peanut butter parfait,
tahini salted caramel and
broken baklava

Golestan Palace, Tehran

Like many people around the world, all I knew about Iran was either what Western media wanted me to know or embellished tales of the great Persian Empire in all of its opulence and glory.

What I found was something different again. Certainly, I did find a place of profound beauty and elegance steeped in historical and religious grandeur, with guardians of a cuisine that was like no other I had encountered during my spice journey thus far. But that's where my preconceived and rather stereotypical view of the Iranian people ended.

The food was exciting. Sweet dried and preserved fruits, sour pomegranate dishes studded with walnuts and perfumed with fragrant spices that seemed to subtly unlock the hidden flavours of the dishes. And techniques for cooking perfect rice that remain unchallenged by any other cuisine. We feasted on smoked rice dishes, sweet rice dishes and witnessed a skill for baking an inch-thick, maddeningly crisp crust on rice called tadek, which blew me away. We refreshed ourselves with crazy frozen rice noodle desserts that can be traced back to 400 BC. Rice and noodles— essential ingredients liberally sprinkled with Iranian food magic.

Some of the best 'one pot dishes' I've ever tasted were in Iran—a simple technique, yet producing balanced and exciting flavour profiles that tap into all the senses. For me this type of dish not only sums up Iranian food, but it shows the skill in which flavour is layered and balanced to achieve perfection. It captured my imagination, as did perfectly cooked Iranian flat bread: bloody good on its own; better piled with fresh fragrant herbs, pickles, saffron, spices, beans, meat and nuts, all coming together in a kind of DIY platter that really did it for me. This is real food, cooked by real people. And, in a nutshell, that's what I loved about Iran.

Sadly, I had very few great 'restaurant' experiences in Iran; it seemed to me that all the best cooking was done behind closed doors, in people's homes with their families. To be honest, that is the story of most of the places I travel to, but here the divide between what you enjoy at home and what was on offer in a restaurant seemed particularly wide.

Some people may look at Middle Eastern food and say it is all the same, which is like saying all Asian food is the same. Iranian food is not Middle Eastern—it is Persian

and it is as diverse, exciting and challenging as any other of the great cuisines of the world. Travelling through this huge country, I found food cultures that really reflected their surroundings. In the Persian Gulf there was a true Pakistani–Emirati feel to the food: exotic seafood combined with sour notes from tamarind and a little more heat than in other parts of Iran; and almost curry-style dishes that I absolutely loved, completed with the subtle refinement of Persian elegance.

Intricate and artistic spicing and cooking techniques in Shiraz not only pushed Iranian food to another level among its Middle Eastern neighbours, but also somehow embodied the graceful and laid-back nature of the city's people. There is definitely something in the air in this town, with its calming and picturesque vistas that all seemed to reflect the poetry of the great Persian poet Hafez, who called this city home.

In Esfahan and Yazd, breathtaking architecture and Islamic grandeur are reflected in the palaces and mosques, and ancient Persian romance is told through stories woven in silk rugs and paintings. All of it converges to captivate your imagination of this once great and all-conquering Persian Empire.

Having spent time in Iran it now strikes me as a tragedy that we in the West have recently pigeon-holed Iran and cast it aside. Underneath all the bureaucracy and political unrest are beautiful people who are proud of their history, food and country.

I am not the kind of person to take a political stand on a cause, or to publicly express an opinion about a complex situation, but I can say that the perception of the Iranian people I had when I left Australia, and the new-found respect, admiration and love for both the people and the country that I came back with, has shaped my life and opened my eyes to a larger world than that which is broadcast on CNN. ✖

*Underneath all the bureaucracy and political unrest are beautiful people who are proud of their history, food and country.*

Preparation time: 10 minutes plus 1 week pickling • Cooking time: 15 minutes • Serves: 6

# EGGPLANT PICKLE WITH BLACK PEPPER AND GREEN CHILLI

**One of the greatest things I learnt in Shiraz is that food is not just something to fill you up, enjoy, and move on—in that ancient city, cooking was entwined with the whole Shirazi and Persian culture. Food imitates art, art is influenced by the poets, and the poets are inspired by the seasons and beauty of nature. It is all one.**

**This dish is so simple, but when I watched it being made and saw the delicacy of the spices being added, I began to understand the subtlety of sweet and sour notes from the sugar and vinegar, and I fell in love with it. My interpretation tones the dish down a little from the original and softens the heat and vinegar flavours.**

- 1 kg (2 lb 4 oz) Lebanese (long thin) eggplants (aubergines), sliced 1 cm (½ inch) thick
- 1 litre (35 fl oz/4 cups) good quality red wine vinegar
- 6 garlic cloves, sliced
- 6 green chillies, split, plus 1 extra, thinly sliced
- 2 tablespoons ground turmeric
- 2 tablespoons ground cumin
- 2 tablespoons ground coriander
- 200 g (7 oz) honey
- 200 g (7 oz) light brown sugar
- splash of olive oil
- 10 mint leaves
- 10 coriander (cilantro) leaves
- 1 tablespoon coriander seeds

Combine the eggplant slices, red wine vinegar, garlic, split chillies, spices, honey and sugar in a large saucepan. Add 2 litres (70 fl oz/8 cups) of water, place over high heat and bring to the boil. Reduce to a simmer and cook for 10 minutes or until the eggplant is tender but not falling apart. Remove from the heat and leave to cool to room temperature.

Transfer to a large sterilised jar and leave in the pantry for at least a week.

Place the pickled eggplant into a mixing bowl, add some olive oil and toss through, put the remaining ingredients on top and serve.

*Notes* The eggplant pickle needs a week in the pantry before it can be used.

Serve as part of a meze platter or with the Slow-roasted lamb shoulder with nomads' jewelled yoghurt and nigella seed bread on page 82.

Salt Lake, Iran

# QUAIL EGG KEFTA TABRIZ

What I really love about this dish is the way the minced chickpeas and potatoes lift the kefta and lighten the whole mix. There are so many versions of kefta throughout the Middle East and to be honest most of them taste fairly similar. Only the spicing changes and their technique of cooking. This kefta from Tabriz was really different. Soft, light, moist and the introduction of the egg in the middle and the freshness of the tarragon really made it something special.

Put the potatoes in a saucepan and cover with cold water. Cook over medium heat for about 15 minutes or until tender. Drain, then place in a bowl with the chickpeas and mash. Set aside.

Bring another saucepan of water to the boil. Add the quail eggs and cook for 2½ minutes, then remove and refresh in iced water. Very carefully peel the shells and discard. Set aside the eggs.

Combine the two minces in a large mixing bowl. Add the mashed potato and chickpea mixture, the tarragon, turmeric, flour and 80 ml (2½ fl oz/⅓ cup) of the saffron water. Mix very well and then divide into 16 balls.

Dampen the palm of your hand with some water, flatten a ball of mince into your palm. Place a cooked and peeled quail egg inside and then cover with the mince mixture to encase the egg. Repeat this process with the rest of the mince mixture and eggs. Set aside.

Put the stock, tomato paste and remaining saffron water in a saucepan over high heat and bring to the boil. Remove from the heat.

Heat the olive oil in a wide-based saucepan over medium–high heat. Add the onion and sauté until translucent. Add the mince balls and cook for a few minutes, turning regularly, until coloured evenly on all sides. Add the risoni and then cover with some of the saffron stock and carefully stir, being careful not to break the balls. Continue adding the stock, a ladle at a time, stirring occasionally, for 15–20 minutes or until the kefta are cooked. Add the butter to the pan, remove from the heat, and stir through. Check the seasoning, then serve immediately.

200 g (7 oz) potatoes, peeled and cut into even-sized pieces

400 g (14 oz) tinned chickpeas, rinsed and drained

16 quail eggs

640 g (1 lb 7 oz) lean minced (ground) lamb

640 g (1 lb 7 oz) lean minced (ground) chicken

small handful tarragon, chopped

1 teaspoon ground turmeric

110 g (3¾ oz/¾ cup) strong flour

500 ml (17 fl oz/2 cups) saffron water*

2 litres (70 fl oz/8 cups) chicken stock

2 tablespoons tomato paste (concentrated purée)

2 tablespoons olive oil

1 brown onion, diced

200 g (7 oz) dried risoni

2½ tablespoons butter

# SLOW-ROASTED LAMB SHOULDER WITH NOMADS' JEWELLED YOGHURT AND NIGELLA SEED BREAD

Travelling along the windy desert road from Esfahan to the Caspian Sea was a hard and long journey—such a huge country with so much untouched countryside that it is easy to get lost in the never-ending and always changing surroundings. During a pit stop I stumbled across a family of nomads who live solely off the land and what they can grow, forage or preserve.

Everything around them was used to the fullest potential, little fires in their tents that served both as a heating source and as a way of cooking breads and meat. Chickens laying eggs that will later become dinner, cheese from the very few cattle they owned and on straw woven racks fruit and berries drying out in the dessert sun to be preserved for the long treks ahead.

Here's a dish they shared with me, with a touch of desert magic.

### SLOW-ROASTED LAMB SHOULDER

Peel the garlic cloves and crush them using a mortar and pestle until smooth. Add the anchovies and continue to crush to a smooth paste. Add the sabaht baharat and olive oil and stir to combine well.

Lightly score the lamb shoulder and smear the marinade all over the lamb. Place in a snug-fitting dish and cover with plastic wrap. Transfer to the fridge and leave to marinate for a day or two to let the flavours of the paste really develop.

Preheat the oven to 90°C (195°F/Gas ½).

Remove the marinated lamb from the fridge and transfer into a roasting tin. Cover tightly with baking paper then foil. Cook for 12 hours or until the meat falls from the bone.

### NOMADS' JEWELLED YOGHURT

Soak the berries and currants in hot tap water for a couple of hours, then drain and set aside.

Place the yoghurt in a serving bowl and garnish with all the ingredients.

### NIGELLA SEED BREAD

Put the flour, yeast, sugar, olive oil and salt into the bowl of an electric stand mixer and combine. Attach the hook attachment, set to medium speed and gradually add 310 ml (10¾ fl oz/1¼ cups) of lukewarm water and mix for 5 minutes

## Slow-roasted lamb shoulder

2 garlic bulbs

4 anchovy fillets

2 tablespoons sabaht baharat* (Lebanese 7 spice)

splash of extra virgin olive oil

1 lamb shoulder, bone in (about 1.1 kg/2 lb 7 oz)

## Nomads' jewelled yoghurt

80 g (2¾ oz) goji berries

50 g (1¾ oz) inkle berries

40 g (1½ oz) barberries

60 g (2¼ oz) dried currants

300 g (10½ oz) Greek-style yoghurt

50 g (1¾ oz) pepitas (pumpkin seeds), toasted

50 g (1¾ oz) sunflower seeds, toasted

50 g (1¾ oz) pomegranate seeds

2 dried apricots, finely diced

2 medjool dates, finely diced

40 g (1½ oz) candied orange and lemon peel (see note)

## Nigella seed bread

450 g (1 lb/3 cups) plain (all-purpose) flour, plus extra for dusting

7 g (⅕ oz) dried yeast

1 teaspoon sugar

60 ml (2 fl oz/¼ cup) olive oil, plus extra to drizzle

1 teaspoon salt flakes, plus extra to season

4 tablespoons nigella seeds

4 tablespoons coriander seeds

4 tablespoons cumin seeds

or until the dough is smooth. Alternatively you can make this dough by hand on your work surface. Put the flour on your surface, make a well in the centre, add the yeast, sugar, olive oil and salt and knead by hand. This should take 6–10 minutes to become smooth.

Place the dough in a bowl, cover with a tea towel (dish towel) and leave to rest for 30 minutes to double in size.

Line a baking tray with baking paper.

Remove the dough from the bowl and place on a floured work surface. Knock back the dough and separate into 8 even-sized portions. Knead each portion into a ball and make divots in the dough using your thumb. Transfer onto the prepared tray and drizzle with olive oil. Combine the seeds in a bowl, scatter them over the dough and season with some more sea salt. Rest again for about 15 minutes to double in size.

Preheat the oven to 190°C (375°F/Gas 5).

Put the bread in the oven and cook for 10–12 minutes, until golden. Keep warm.

## TO SERVE

Serve the slow-roasted lamb shoulder with the nomads' jewelled yoghurt and the warm nigella seed bread.

Note This dish does require a bit of effort, and needs to be started 2 days in advance, but trust me, it's worth it.

Candied orange and lemon peel are available from specialty food stores and online.

Slow-roasted lamb shoulder with nomads' jewelled yoghurt and nigella seed bread

# ROASTED PORK BELLY WITH FENUGREEK SALAD AND ROAST GARLIC VINAIGRETTE

**Salt and pork belly is a real match made in heaven. Now pork isn't something you're going to find in Iran, but as I walked through the pomegranate fields and saw wild fenugreek growing all around me I couldn't help but think that these sweet, sour and fresh notes would work amazingly well together and really cut the fatness of a pork dish. So here it is.**

Preheat the oven to 110°C (225°F/Gas ½).

Using a mortar and pestle, crush the garlic into a fine paste with the aid of some salt. Add the anchovies and continue to crush until smooth. Add the sabaht baharat and olive oil and stir through well.

Rub the bottom of the pork belly generously with the garlic mixture. Place the pork on a wire rack in a baking dish, add 300 ml (10½ fl oz) of water to the dish to provide some moisture, then place in the oven and cook for 8 hours.

Meanwhile, to make the roast garlic vinaigrette, put the garlic on a baking tray and place in the oven with the pork. Roast for 30 minutes, or until soft and fragrant. Remove the garlic from the oven and squeeze out the soft roasted cloves into a small mixing bowl. Combine with the molasses, lemon juice and a pinch of salt, and emulsify with the olive oil. Reserve until required.

Increase the oven temperature to 210°C (410°F/Gas 6–7) and cook the pork belly for a final 10–15 minutes or until the skin is crisp and crackling.

Meanwhile, to make the fenugreek salad, combine the ingredients in a bowl. Dress with the roast garlic vinaigrette.

To serve, carve the pork into individual portions. Place on four plates with the fenugreek salad and serve.

8 garlic cloves
pinch of salt flakes
6 anchovy fillets, rinsed
2 tablespoons sabaht baharat*
   (Lebanese 7 spice)
2½ tablespoons extra virgin olive oil
800 g (1 lb 12 oz) piece of pork belly

## Roast garlic vinaigrette

2 garlic bulbs
1½ tablespoons pomegranate
   molasses*
squeeze of lemon juice
200 ml (7 fl oz) olive oil

## Fenugreek salad

large handful fenugreek (or purslane,
   mache or tatsoi)
5 French shallots, thinly shaved
3 radishes, thinly shaved
60 g (2¼ oz/¼ cup) pomegranate
   seeds (optional)
80 g (2¾ oz/½ cup) pine nuts,
   toasted
60 g (2¼ oz/¼ cup) goji berries,
   soaked in hot water for 10 minutes
60 g (2¼ oz/¼ cup) inkle berries,
   soaked in hot water for 10 minutes

# PISTACHIO AND BARBERRY NOUGAT DOUGHNUTS WITH ORANGE BLOSSOM SYRUP

**This dish pays homage to the syrupy sweet desserts I found in Iran. Mega tasty with a little gooey surprise in the middle.**

Using an electric stand mixer with the whisk attachment, whip the egg whites at a moderate speed until they begin to foam and hold stiff peaks. Continue to whisk at low speed while you make the syrup.

Combine the sugar, glucose and 60 ml (2 fl oz/ ¼ cup) of water in a saucepan over medium–high heat. Continue to cook until the mixture reaches soft ball stage—to test if the syrup is ready drop a small amount into a shallow bowl of cold water to cool it down. If you have a kitchen thermometer, the syrup will be ready when the temperature reaches 115–118°C (about 240°F).

Line a baking tin with baking paper. Pour the sugar syrup slowly into the egg mixture and continue beating on low for around 20 minutes or until the mixture is cool. Add the barberries and pistachios and beat until just combined. Pour the nougat onto the prepared tray and allow to set for 10 minutes.

Mix the cornflour and icing sugar together in a small bowl then spread over a tray. Roll the nougat into thirty 1.5 cm (⅝ inch) balls and place on the tray. Roll in the cornflour and icing sugar mixture to coat. Cover and set aside.

To make the batter, mix the yeast and 250 ml (9 fl oz/1 cup) of water in a large bowl. Fold through the flour, sugar and salt, then cover with a tea towel (dish towel) and leave to prove in a warm place for 30 minutes or until doubled in size.

To make the orange blossom syrup, put the honey in a small saucepan and bring to the boil over high heat. As soon as it begins to boil remove from the heat and add the orange blossom water. Set aside.

Heat the canola oil in a deep heavy-based frying pan or deep-fryer until shimmering. If you have a kitchen thermometer, the oil will be ready when the temperature reaches 170°C (325°F). Scoop out some dough, about half the size of your palm, and press a ball of nougat into the centre. Turn your hand, and squeeze your fist over the surface of the hot oil. The batter should come out between your thumb and index finger into the shape of a round ball. Pinch or use a knife to cut the dough encasing the nougat, allowing the doughnut to gently drop into the hot oil. Repeat to make the remaining doughnuts.

Cook in batches (you don't want to overcrowd the pan) for about 5–6 minutes until golden brown. Drain on paper towel.

Drizzle the warm orange blossom syrup over the hot doughnuts and serve.

### Pistachio and barberry nougat
2 egg whites
500 g (1 lb 2 oz) caster (superfine) sugar
350 g (12 oz) liquid glucose*
35 g (1¼ oz/¼ cup) barberries (or cranberries)
70 g (2½ oz/½ cup) pistachio nuts
2 tablespoons cornflour (cornstarch)
2 tablespoons icing (confectioners') sugar

### Doughnut batter
15 g (½ oz) dried yeast
300 g (10½ oz/2 cups) plain (all-purpose) flour
2 teaspoons sugar
pinch of salt flakes
canola oil, for deep-frying

### Orange blossom syrup
300 g (10½ oz) honey
100 ml (3½ fl oz) orange blossom water*

# SAFFRON ROASTED PEACHES WITH SAFFRON FAIRY FLOSS

I'd always thought of saffron as one of the most feminine, gentle and prestigious spices in the Middle Eastern kitchen. I remember softly walking through the saffron fields in Yazd, being so careful not to step on any of the little saffron flower bulbs, watching old men and women crouched over, with hands that were as worn and cracked as the dry earth of the Iranian desert, seeing the love and dedication they put into picking every strand of saffron by hand. The experience will stay with me forever and makes me appreciate this beautiful product even more.

Preheat the oven to 180°C (350°F/Gas 4).

Place the peaches in a baking dish and season with the saffron, vanilla, cinnamon and bay leaf. Sprinkle over the caster sugar and pour over the saffron water. Roast in the oven for 20–25 minutes, or until the peaches feel soft and cooked through when pierced with a sharp knife.

Place the peaches on four serving plates. Drizzle over the pan juices, add some saffron fairy floss and serve.

Notes You can cut the peaches in half, if you like, or use another stone fruit.
Saffron fairy floss is available from specialist Middle Eastern grocery shops.

4 peaches
pinch of saffron threads
1 vanilla bean, split and scraped
1 cinnamon stick
2 bay leaves, torn
150 g (5½ oz/⅔ cup) caster
    (superfine) sugar
200 ml (7 fl oz) saffron water*
150 g (5½ oz) saffron fairy floss
    (pashmak)

Turkey and I have a lot of history, admittedly none of which is actually firsthand. I grew up with stories on my father's knee about the Great Siege of Malta in 1565 when the Ottoman Empire tried to take my ancestral home only to be defeated by the Knights Hospitaller, the legendary warriors of Malta.

These dramatic tales of how Spanish foot soldiers and the local Maltese fought off the Sultan and his Ottoman subjects, filled my little heart with a phenomenal sense of national pride: that I was descended from people from a tiny island in the Mediterranean, who could stand up against the biggest empire in the world at the time, and win.

More recently, in 1915, but under much the same heroic and heartbreaking circumstances, World War I Australian and New Zealand (ANZAC) troops were ill-fatedly deployed at the Gallipoli Peninsula. What they found waiting for them was a heavily armed and strategically positioned Turkish force, dug in and ready to defend at all costs. During that eight-month ordeal a staggering 44,000 Allies and 85,000 Turkish soldiers died, but the legacy it forged was a deep-seated respect, admiration and generational bond. The passion, character and camaraderie of both ANZAC and Turkish troops cemented the connection we Australians still hold with Turkey and her people today.

So what excites me the most about Turkey is probably not what excites most people when they go there, although there is an undeniable aura to the place, especially when you walk through the streets of Istanbul at sunset as the sun gently kisses the tops of the ancient and spectacular palaces dotted along the mighty Bosphorus. I remember sitting in Mandabatmaz, my absolute favourite coffee shop, watching the world drift by and seeing beaming rays of light through the city streets gradually fading into darkness, and I was captivated by all the romance, history and greatness that Turkey once was under the Ottomans and still is today.

Since then I have developed a deep love affair with Istanbul. She has stolen a little piece of my heart and I can't wait to return with Maha so we can both experience all the hidden secrets she still has in store for me.

*There is an undeniable aura to the place, especially when you walk through the streets of Istanbul at sunset.*

Some say that Turkey's true beauty lies in its Aegean coastline or vast Anatolian plains. Others are captivated by the otherworldly natural beauty of Cappadocia and the fairytale chimney stacks of Goreme. For others, it's when you venture into the brooding Black Sea region of the north and experience a countryside not stereotypically Turkish—rolling green hills, waterfalls and a cuisine influenced enormously by its Georgian immigrants. But for me, the most exciting thing about Turkey isn't its fascinating history or exotic places, it is the bounty of riches it possesses in its produce. At every turn in this great land you see all the ingredients needed to become a leader in global gastronomy.

I was blown away by the quality and diversity of Turkish produce—spices, flours, oils, meats, fruits, vegetables, artisan specialty products and techniques for preparing them that have been perfected over hundreds, if not thousands, of years—forming the backbone not only of Turkish cuisine but of Turkish culture. There is so much untapped wealth here it is hard to know where to begin, but the diverse landscape and cuisine of Turkey means that the scope of what can be grown and how it can be cooked, is enormous. Until now, the only thing holding Turkey back, has been Turkey.

Much like the surrounding countries in the Middle East, Turkish food has had restricted growth. Whether it be political, religious, geographical, cultural or historical, much of this region's food has not developed steadily over the centuries. This isn't always a bad thing—it shows purity in the cuisine and a love for something that has been perfected over thousands of years—but if you look at past and current food innovators, and their deep respect for food history, there is a potential for Turkey to develop her national cuisine to a new level and become an international force.

Here you have a rich and diverse food culture, producers and chefs who are forward thinking and adventurous, and a society that is hungry for change as well as being passionate about its heritage. All Turkey needs to do is rally her troops, fly under a united flag and cook without fear or hesitation, and the world will be hers to conquer once more. ✖

*Here you have a rich and diverse food culture, producers and chefs who are forward thinking and adventurous.*

# CURED SALMON WITH BEETROOT MAYONNAISE, PUMPKIN PURÉE AND FENNEL VINAIGRETTE

Seafood is big on the menu all down the Aegean coast of Turkey, and when it is this high quality it is pretty obvious why. Curing fish is a technique that dates back millennia on both sides of the Aegean in Greece and Turkey, and it is this tradition along with the local fresh produce that inspired me to make this dish.

Preheat the oven to 180°C (350°F/Gas 4).

Roughly chop the carrots. Put the carrots, salt, sugar and cardamom in a food processor and mix until coarsely puréed. Place half the mixture in the base of a large dish and lay the salmon on top. Cover well with the remaining mixture. Cover with plastic wrap and refrigerate for 3–4 hours. Wash off the cure as well as any bloodline and cut into 1 cm (½ inch) thick slices.

Meanwhile, cover a baking tray with the rock salt. Place the beetroot on top and cook for 45–60 minutes until tender. Remove from the oven and set aside to cool. When cool enough to handle, peel the skin off, place in a bowl and purée using a hand-held stick blender. Reserve.

Place the egg and egg yolks in a food processor with the mustard and lemon juice. Process until smooth. With the machine still running, slowly trickle in the blended oil until it is emulsified.

Mix equal parts of beetroot purée and mayonnaise. Reserve any that is left over for another use. Transfer the beetroot mayonnaise into a bowl and refrigerate until required.

To make the pumpkin purée, grate the pumpkin using the largest holes of a cheese grater. Heat the butter in a saucepan over medium–low heat, then add the pumpkin. Cover with a lid and cook for 10 minutes, stirring occasionally. When the pumpkin is tender, add the cream, stir through, then transfer into the food processor and blend until smooth. Set aside.

To make the fennel vinaigrette, place the vinegar and sugar in a saucepan and bring to the boil. Set aside to cool then add the micro fennel.

To serve, place a slice of salmon on each serving plate. Dress with the fennel vinaigrette, extra virgin olive oil and some salt. Add dollops of the beetroot mayonnaise and pumpkin purée. Garnish with some fennel fronds. Serve immediately.

**Note** If you can't get micro fennel, slice baby fennel into thin lengths.

## Cured salmon
5 carrots, peeled
130 g (4½ oz/1 cup) table salt
220 g (7¾ oz/1 cup) caster (superfine) sugar
70 g (2½ oz/¾ cup) cardamom pods, cracked open and toasted
1 side sashimi-grade salmon (about 800 g/1 lb 12 oz), pin boned, skin removed

## Beetroot mayonnaise
500 g (1 lb 2 oz) rock salt
500 g (1 lb 2 oz) beetroot (beets)
1 egg
5 egg yolks
2 tablespoons dijon mustard
2½ tablespoons lemon juice
600 ml (21 fl oz) blended oil (50:50 vegetable oil and olive oil)

## Pumpkin purée
500 g (1 lb 2 oz) jap or kent pumpkin (winter squash)
80 g (2¾ oz) butter
150 ml (5 fl oz) thickened (whipping) cream

## Fennel vinaigrette
300 ml (10½ fl oz) chardonnay vinegar
300 g (10½ oz) brown sugar
8 micro fennel, thinly sliced, plus extra fronds, to serve

splash of extra virgin olive oil
pinch of salt flakes

Preparation time: 30 minutes plus 20 minutes chilling • Cooking time: 30 minutes • Serves: 4

# SCALLOP-FILLED ZUCCHINI FLOWERS WITH SMOKED EEL DRESSING AND ORANGE AND CORIANDER CRUMB

**I found flowers growing wild throughout Turkey, and in Bodrum it inspired me to use vegetable flowers in my cooking. This dish is one of the results.**

Put the rice in a small saucepan with enough water to cover by 1 cm (½ inch). Bring to the boil, cover with a lid and cook for 12–15 minutes until the water is absorbed and the rice is plump and tender.

Heat the olive oil in a frying pan over medium–high heat. Add the onion and sauté for a few minutes until translucent. Add the pine nuts, cooked rice and lemon zest. Stir through and then remove from the heat. Add the scallops, cheeses and mint and stir through.

Fill the zucchini flowers with the scallop filling and gently fold or twist the opening shut. Place on a tray, cover with plastic wrap and refrigerate.

To make the crumb, combine the orange zest, breadcrumbs and coriander seeds in a shallow bowl. Lightly coat the filled zucchini flowers in the flour, dip in the beaten egg, then roll in the breadcrumbs to evenly cover. Transfer onto a plate, cover with plastic wrap and refrigerate to rest.

Meanwhile, to make the smoked eel dressing, flake the eel meat into a mixing bowl, add the remaining ingredients and check the seasoning. Set aside.

Pour some sunflower oil into a deep frying pan, about 4 cm (1½ inches) deep, then heat over medium–high heat until it shimmers. If you have a kitchen thermometer, the oil will be ready when the temperature reaches 180°C (350°F). Alternatively, use a deep-fryer. Remove the zucchini flowers from the fridge and carefully add to the pan, a few at a time, then cook for 2–3 minutes until all the sides are golden brown, turning as necessary. Drain on paper towel.

Divide the zucchini flowers between four serving plates. Drizzle with the smoked eel dressing and serve immediately.

**Note** Pumpkin flowers work best for this dish but aren't always easy to find so we've used zucchini flowers instead, as an easy replacement.

### Scallop-filled zucchini flowers

110 g (3¾ oz/½ cup) baldo rice (or arborio rice)
2 tablespoons olive oil
1 brown onion, finely diced
2 tablespoons pine nuts, toasted
zest of 1 lemon
12 scallops, roe removed, quartered
80 g (2¾ oz) haloumi cheese, finely grated
120 g (4¼ oz) kefalograviera (or parmesan cheese), finely grated
small handful mint, leaves picked and torn
12 zucchini (courgette) flowers, buds removed (see note)
sunflower oil, for deep-frying

### Orange and coriander crumb

zest of 1 orange
300 g (10½ oz/2⅔ cups) dry breadcrumbs
2½ tablespoons coriander seeds, crushed
plain (all-purpose) flour, for dusting
2 eggs, beaten

### Smoked eel dressing

½ smoked eel (about 200 g/7 oz), meat picked from bone and skin
2 French shallots, finely diced
2 tablespoons sherry vinegar
250 ml (9 fl oz/1 cup) olive oil
1 tablespoon red Aleppo pepper* (pul biber)
large handful flat-leaf (Italian) parsley leaves, roughly torn

# CEMEN CURED BLUE EYE PASTIRMA WITH TARAMASALATA

A popular process for preserving meat, called pastirma in Turkey, involves covering meat in a spice paste (cemen) and leaving it to cure. It's a technique that many nationalities lay claim to around the Mediterranean and Baltic seas, but, to be honest, I don't care where it originated as long as it tastes great, and the pastirma I had in Turkey was AMAZING!

Curing meat can be a long and risky process if you get it wrong. This is a really simple recipe that has all the big flavours of a traditional meat pastirma, but brings some new life to it with the introduction of fish. It is a lot easier to make as well.

Combine all the dry curing ingredients with the orange zest in a large bowl.

Place half the mixture on the base of a large rectangular tray. Place the fish on top and cover with the remaining mixture, pressing it down onto the blue eye. Cover with plastic wrap then place in the fridge and allow to cure for 6 hours.

Quickly rinse the fish under cold running water to remove any excess curing mixture, leaving a thin layer of spice still attached. Slice the blue eye into 5 mm (¼ inch) slices and keep refrigerated until required.

Put the bread in a bowl, cover with 300 ml (10½ fl oz) of water and leave to soak for 10 minutes. Remove the bread and squeeze out the water.

Blend the onion in a food processor. Add the soaked bread and process until smooth. Add the cod roe and lemon juice, and process until smooth. While the motor is running, slowly drizzle in the olive oil, a little at a time. Season the taramasalata with salt to taste. (See note.)

Place slices of fish in the middle of a large platter. Add dollops of taramasalata, chives, radish, beach banana, if using, and micro cress, if using, and serve.

**Note** Beach banana is a ground running creeper with fleshy leaves, which have a light, sweet, salty taste. It is available in punnets from specialty markets and food stores.

Instead of taramasalata, you could also serve the cemen cured blue eye with Kewpie mayonnaise.

## Cured blue eye pastirma
80 g (2¾ oz) ground fenugreek
80 g (2¾ oz) smoked paprika
2½ tablespoons ground coriander
2½ tablespoons ground cumin
160 g (5½ oz) salt flakes
160 g (5½ oz) sugar
zest of 1 orange
1 side blue eye (trevalla), skin, bone
   and bloodline removed

## Taramasalata
4 slices white bread, crusts removed
½ onion, roughly chopped
100 g (3½ oz) white cod roe paste
2 tablespoons lemon juice
500 ml (17 fl oz/2 cups) olive oil
pinch of salt flakes

handful chives, cut into 2 cm
   (¾ inch) lengths
1 radish, very thinly sliced
small handful beach banana
   (optional) (see note)
micro cress (optional)

# VILLAGE-STYLE FETA BOREK WITH SMOKED EGGPLANT MAYONNAISE

When I was in Turkey I picked up a great trick for making borek, using sparkling mineral water with the oil to brush over the pastries. This really is the difference between the amazing boreks I had in Turkey and the ones I'd been cooking at home. Another tip is to make sure you add a little salt to the egg mix—it adds a bit of crunch to the finished product.

Fry off the diced sucuk in a large frying pan, over medium heat, until crispy and golden. Remove the sucuk from the heat and stir through the feta and parsley.

Combine the olive oil and salt in small bowl with the mineral water and stir.

Carefully cut each sheet of pastry into 8 triangle shapes. Place a tablespoon of the sucuk mixture in the middle of each pastry triangle, about 2 cm (¾ inch) from the edge. Brush the pastry with the olive oil and water mixture, roll the filling tightly into the pastry, folding in the sides to create a cylinder shape, to make 16 boreks.

To make the smoked eggplant mayonnaise, place the whole eggplants over a gas flame, or on a barbecue grill, and cook until the skin is charred and the eggplant is soft. Set aside to cool, then remove the skin and cut the flesh into rough chunks.

Place the egg and egg yolks in a food processor with the mustard and lemon juice. Process until smooth. With the machine still running, slowly trickle in the blended oil until it is all emulsified. Add the eggplant, red Aleppo pepper, lemon zest, tahini and salt to taste, and continue to process until smooth.

Pour some canola oil into a deep frying pan, about 4 cm (1½ inches) deep, then heat over medium–high heat until it shimmers. If you have a kitchen thermometer, the oil will be ready when the temperature reaches 180°C (350°F). Alternatively, use a deep-fryer. Carefully add the boreks to the pan and cook for 2–3 minutes until golden brown. Transfer onto paper towel to drain.

Serve the village-style feta borek hot with the smoked eggplant mayonnaise.

## Feta borek

250 g (9 oz) sucuk sausages*, diced small
150 g (5½ oz) feta cheese, crumbled
handful flat-leaf (Italian) parsley, leaves picked and torn
250 ml (9 fl oz/1 cup) olive oil
2 tablespoons salt flakes
125 ml (4 fl oz/½ cup) sparkling mineral water
2 sheets yufka pastry (or filo pastry)
canola oil, for deep-frying

## Smoked eggplant mayonnaise

2 eggplants (aubergines)
1 egg
5 egg yolks
2 tablespoons dijon mustard
2½ tablespoons lemon juice
1 litre (35 fl oz/4 cups) blended oil (50:50 vegetable oil and olive oil)
1 tablespoon red Aleppo pepper* (pul biber)
zest of 1 lemon
2 tablespoons tahini*
pinch of salt flakes

# STUFFED MUSSELS WITH PRESERVED LEMON DRESSING

Everywhere you go in Istanbul there is a mussel dish on the menu. Two of the best I experienced had to have been fried mussels on a stick, and stuffed mussels with rice. This dish brings together elements of both in a really tasty combination.

First, cook the mussels. Heat the olive oil and butter in a saucepan over medium–high heat, add the French shallots, garlic, thyme and bay leaf, and sauté for a few minutes until translucent. Add the mussels and white wine and cook for 30–60 seconds or until the mussels start to open. Strain into a colander to cool over a bowl and set aside.

To make the rice filling, put the rice in a saucepan with enough water to cover by 1 cm (½ inch). Bring to the boil, cover with a lid and cook for 12–15 minutes until the water has been absorbed and the rice is plump and tender.

Melt the butter in a frying pan over medium heat. Add the pine nuts and stir until golden brown. Add the currants and sabaht baharat and stir through. Tear the parsley leaves and add to the pan with the cooked rice, season with salt, then turn out onto a tray and leave to cool.

Remove the mussels from the shells, make sure the beards have been removed and fill with the rice filling. Refrigerate for at least 30 minutes.

Put the cornflour and 150 g (5½ oz/1 cup) of the plain flour into a mixing bowl and combine. Using a whisk, slowly add the mineral water to make a smooth pouring consistency batter, but make sure the batter is thick enough to coat the mussels.

To make the preserved lemon dressing, combine the ingredients in a small bowl and set aside.

Pour some sunflower oil into a deep frying pan, about 4 cm (1½ inches) deep, then heat over medium–high heat until it shimmers. If you have a kitchen thermometer, the oil will be ready when the temperature reaches 180°C (350°F). Alternatively, use a deep-fryer.

Coat the stuffed mussels with the remaining 75 g (2½ oz/½ cup) of flour, dip in the tempura batter, then shake off the excess. Carefully place the battered mussels into the pan, a few at a time, and cook for 1–2 minutes, then remove and place on paper towel to soak up the oil. Repeat with the remaining mussels.

Place the cooked mussels on a plate and dress with the preserved lemon dressing. Serve immediately.

## Mussels
2 tablespoons olive oil
2 tablespoons butter
2 French shallots, thinly sliced
1 garlic clove, thinly sliced
5 thyme sprigs
1 bay leaf, torn
1 kg (2 lb 4 oz) mussels, cleaned
250 ml (9 fl oz/1 cup) dry white wine

## Rice filling
110 g (3¾ oz/½ cup) baldo rice
    (or arborio rice)
2 tablespoons butter
2 tablespoons pine nuts
2 tablespoons dried currants
1 tablespoon sabaht baharat*
    (Lebanese 7 spice)
small handful flat-leaf (Italian)
    parsley, leaves picked
pinch of salt

## Tempura batter
250 g (9 oz/2 cups) cornflour
    (cornstarch)
225 g (8 oz/1½ cups) plain
    (all-purpose) flour
500 ml (17 fl oz/2 cups) mineral water
    (or soda water)
sunflower oil, for deep-frying

## Preserved lemon dressing
1 tablespoon finely diced French
    shallot
2 tablespoons diced preserved
    lemon peel
1 teaspoon black Aleppo pepper*
    (pul biber)
80 ml (2½ fl oz/⅓ cup) olive oil
2 tablespoons sherry vinegar

# MOREL, SILVERBEET AND DUCK GOZLEME WITH MOREL BUTTER

**I was really surprised to find so much game, mushrooms and fresh produce in the hills surrounding Fethiye and around the Bodrum Peninsula. It really wasn't the Turkey I was expecting to find and reminded me a lot more of Europe than Anatolia. This gozleme dish unites a lot of them.**

To make the gozleme dough, put the flour, salt, sugar, olive oil and 325 ml (11 fl oz) of water into the bowl of an electric stand mixer. Attach the dough hook and mix at low speed for 7 minutes or until combined. Cover the bowl with a tea towel (dish towel) and place in a warm spot for 30 minutes to double in size.

To make the morel butter, combine all the ingredients in a food processor and blitz until smooth. Set aside.

To make the morel, silverbeet and duck filling, heat the butter in a frying pan over medium heat. Add the onion and sauté for a few minutes until translucent. Add the morels, bay leaf and rosemary and stir. As the morels become crispier, add the ground cumin and stir through. Tip out onto a tray to cool.

Combine the silverbeet, black cabbage, duck mince, feta, Aleppo pepper and 1 tablespoon of the morel butter with the sautéed ingredients in a large bowl. Mix well, then set aside.

Sprinkle some flour on your work surface and divide the gozleme dough into 10 portions. Roll out the dough portions into 15 cm (6 inch) flat rounds, 2 mm (1/16 inch) thick. Place a good even layer of the duck mix on one half, leaving a 1 cm (1/2 inch) border from the edge of the pastry. Fold over and seal the rim.

Place 2 tablespoons of the remaining morel butter onto a flat grill over medium–high heat (see note). Place a few gozleme on top to cook, brushing the tops with more morel butter. When the pastry is golden, after 2–3 minutes, turn over and cook for a further 2–3 minutes. Repeat with the remaining gozleme.

Serve immediately.

**Note** You can also use a hot pan, barbecue grill or pizza stone to cook the gozleme.

## Gozleme dough
500 g (1 lb 2 oz/3⅓ cups) plain (all-purpose) flour, plus extra for dusting
pinch of salt flakes
pinch of caster (superfine) sugar
splash of olive oil

## Morel butter
50 g (1¾ oz/1 cup) dried morels, soaked for at least 15 minutes
150 g (5½ oz) butter, at room temperature
pinch of salt flakes
2 tablespoons olive oil

## Morel, silverbeet and duck filling
2 tablespoons butter
1 large brown onion, finely chopped
100 g (3½ oz/2 cups) dried morels, soaked for at least 15 minutes, roughly chopped
1 bay leaf, torn
1 rosemary sprig
1 teaspoon ground cumin
3 silverbeet (Swiss chard) leaves, stem removed, finely chopped
3 black cabbage (cavalo nero) leaves, finely chopped
250 g (9 oz) minced (ground) duck
150 g (5½ oz) feta cheese, crumbled
1 tablespoon red Aleppo pepper* (pul biber)

# SMOKED TROUT TRAHANA

**This would have to be where food companies stole the idea for packet soup! This is a great dish with heaps of flavour that I haven't changed very much from the original I tried in Turkey. The smoked rainbow trout is the only substantial difference, helping to lift what was already a superb dish.**

Bring a small saucepan of water to the boil, add the lentils and cook for 15 minutes or until just tender. Drain and set aside.

Bring 1.5 litres (52 fl oz/6 cups) of water to the boil in a saucepan over medium–high heat. Pour 125 ml (4 fl oz/½ cup) of the water from the pan into a bowl and add the trahana, then pour it back into the pan. Stir through for 3–4 minutes, add the butter and season to taste. Set aside.

Combine all the vegetables, the lentils, Aleppo pepper and smoked trout in a mixing bowl. Arrange a small amount in the middle of each serving bowl, scatter the watercress on top, pour over the soup and serve.

**Notes** Trahana is a soup base made from cracked grains and fermented yoghurt which is dried and then ground into a powder. It is available from specialist Middle Eastern grocery shops.

You can substitute smoked salmon for the trout.

55 g (2 oz/¼ cup) puy lentils

150 g (5½ oz/1 cup) trahana (see note)

100 g (3½ oz) butter

1 small celery stalk, finely diced

1 carrot, peeled and finely diced

1 small turnip, peeled and finely diced

1 teaspoon black Aleppo pepper* (pul biber)

150 g (5½ oz) smoked rainbow trout, skin removed, flesh flaked from the bone (see note)

handful watercress, leaves picked

# LAMB SHANK KEBAB

Traditionally, this dish is cooked in a tandoori-style oven that is built into the floor of central Anatolian kitchens. The clay for the pot it is cooked in is sourced from a local river that has a high mineral content and in turn this leaches out a salty, earthy taste into the finished dish. But never fear, this recipe simply cooked in a heavy-based casserole dish produces a beautiful result. It may not have the romance of the original, but it saves you digging up your kitchen floor to build the oven. Enjoy!

Soak the haricot beans and borlotti beans in separate bowls of water overnight. Drain and set aside.

Combine the garlic, rosemary, red Aleppo pepper, 1 tablespoon of the black Aleppo pepper and the salt using a mortar and pestle. Rub the mixture onto the lamb shanks to evenly coat. Place the shanks in a non-metallic bowl, cover with plastic wrap and refrigerate for at least 4 hours to marinate.

Preheat the oven to 160°C (315°F/Gas 2–3).

Seal the lamb shanks in a flameproof casserole dish over medium–high heat, on all sides until golden brown. Add the spices and 2 remaining tablespoons of black Aleppo pepper to the dish and cook for 1 minute. Add the pastes and stir through, then add the carrots and onions, soaked beans and tomatoes. Add the stock to just cover the meat, cover the dish with a lid and cook for 3 hours, or until the meat falls from the bones.

Remove the dish from the oven, stir in the black cabbage, top with the walnuts and lemon zest, and serve.

**Note** Use lamb leg or shoulder if you can't get shanks.

200 g (7 oz/1 cup) dried haricot beans
200 g (7 oz/1 cup) dried borlotti beans
2 garlic bulbs, cloves peeled and crushed
2 rosemary sprigs
1 tablespoon red Aleppo pepper* (pul biber)
3 tablespoons black Aleppo pepper* (pul biber)
pinch of salt flakes
6 lamb shanks (about 300 g/10½ oz each) (see note)
3 cinnamon sticks
1 tablespoon ground cumin
1 tablespoon ground coriander
2 tablespoons capsicum paste*
2 tablespoons tomato paste (concentrated purée)
2 carrots, peeled and quartered
12 cocktail onions
6 vine-ripened tomatoes, quartered
2 litres (70 fl oz/8 cups) lamb stock (or another meat stock)
8 black cabbage (cavolo nero) leaves
70 g (2½ oz) walnuts, toasted and crushed
zest of 1 lemon

Istiklal Avenue, Taksim, Istanbul

# PASTIRMA, PRAWN AND FETA PIDE

Now the debate over who invented the pizza is one I'll leave to others. All I care about is if it is good or not. I love a traditional Neapolitan-style pizza, and Turkish- and Lebanese-style spiced lamb mince flat pizzas are foods that get my heart pumping and are probably responsible for about two kilograms of my belly fat. But I have to admit that Turkish pide at its best is something not to be messed with. Light, airy, crispy pastry that holds together endless amounts of flavour. Sitting by the Bosphorus devouring a fresh pide and washing it down with a few Turkish beers—I can't really think of anything better.

Combine the dough ingredients and 100 ml (3½ fl oz) of lukewarm water in an electric stand mixer. Attach the dough hook and knead for 3–5 minutes at a moderate–high speed, until the dough is smooth and starts to come away from the bowl. Cover with a tea towel (dish towel) and set aside to prove in a warm spot for 30 minutes or until the dough doubles in size.

Combine the prawns, feta, black cabbage, spices, lemon zest and parsley in a large bowl. Cover with plastic wrap and refrigerate until required.

Preheat the oven to 220°C (425°F/Gas 7).

Sprinkle some flour on your work surface. Divide the dough into 2 portions and then use a rolling pin and roll each portion into a rectangle shape. Divide the filling evenly into 2 portions and put these in the middle of each dough portion, then fold over the edges and pinch at either end. Place the pastirma slices down the centre.

Place the pides on a preheated pizza stone or baking tray and cook for 8–10 minutes until golden.

Serve hot with lemon wedges.

Notes You can use dried yeast if fresh yeast is not available. Generally, you require half the quantity of dried yeast.

Pastirma is a Middle Eastern cured meat, available from continental delicatessens and specialist Middle Eastern grocery shops. If pastirma isn't really your thing, you can substitute any other cured meat—Spanish jamon would work as a great replacement.

### Pide dough

5 g (⅛ oz) fresh yeast (see note)

1 teaspoon sugar

150 g (5½ oz/1 cup) strong flour, plus extra for dusting

1 teaspoon salt flakes

10 large raw prawns (shrimp), peeled and deveined, tails removed

150 g (5½ oz) feta cheese, crumbled

5 black cabbage (cavolo nero) leaves, blanched and torn

1 teaspoon black Aleppo pepper* (pul biber)

1 teaspoon fennel seeds

1 teaspoon ground coriander

zest of 1 lemon

large handful flat-leaf (Italian) parsley, leaves picked

100 g (3½ oz) pastirma, cut into 2 mm (1⁄16 inch) slices (see note)

lemon wedges, to serve

Preparation time: 40 minutes • Cooking time: 25 minutes • Serves: 4

# ALI NAZIK LAMB KOFTE WITH EGGPLANT YOGHURT AND BLACK BREAD GARNISH

This is one of the dishes that really defines Turkish food for me. Beautiful coal-grilled lamb with smoky, silky eggplant and a spicy butter sauce. I could eat this dish every day for the rest of my life and be a very happy man. By far the best Ali Nazik dish I tasted was in Gaziantep at one of my all-time favourite restaurants, Imam Cagdas. You can't go to Turkey and not eat there. The baklava served in the street-front pastry shop is the best there is and the food served in the restaurant upstairs is out of this world.

Combine the lamb mince, lamb tail fat, Aleppo pepper and garlic in a bowl and mix well. Divide into 4 even-sized balls and thread onto four skewers in a barrel shape, distributing evenly. Cover with plastic wrap and refrigerate.

Meanwhile, place the whole eggplants over a gas flame or barbecue grill and cook until the skin is well charred and the eggplant is soft. Set aside to cool, then remove the skin and cut the flesh into rough chunks. Transfer into a food processor and blend until smooth (see note).

Combine the puréed eggplant with the yoghurt in a bowl, and then fold through the purslane.

To make the black bread garnish, melt the butter in a frying pan over high heat. When the butter begins to foam, add the capsicum paste and stir well. Roughly break up the black bread and add it to the pan. Add the almonds, Aleppo pepper, lemon juice and parsley, and stir through. Set aside.

Preheat your barbecue grill or hotplate to medium–high. Remove the lamb skewers from the fridge.

Cook the kofte for 3–4 minutes on each side until cooked through evenly. Carefully remove from the skewers and cut each one into 3 pieces.

Pool some eggplant yoghurt onto each serving plate. Add the kofta and top with the bread garnish and pan juices. Serve immediately.

**Note** You can keep the eggplant pieces chunky instead of puréed if you prefer.

### Lamb kofte
250 g (9 oz) minced (ground) lean lamb shoulder
50 g (1¾ oz) lamb tail fat*
1 tablespoon black Aleppo pepper* (pul biber)
1 large garlic clove, crushed

### Eggplant yoghurt
3 eggplants (aubergines)
200 g (7 oz/¾ cup) Greek-style yoghurt
small handful purslane (or fenugreek or mache)

### Black bread garnish
2 tablespoons butter
1 tablespoon capsicum paste*
black bread (see page 124)
50 g (1¾ oz/½ cup) flaked almonds, toasted
1 teaspoon red Aleppo pepper* (pul biber)
squeeze of lemon juice
small handful flat-leaf (Italian) parsley, leaves picked and torn

# BLACK BREAD

Now, this bread recipe isn't traditionally Turkish. The reason I wanted to include it is because, for me, the best meat and kofte is always cooked over coal, but not all of us can have the luxury of having a coal grill set-up. So this bread is the next best thing. When you tear the baked bread and fry it in butter, lemon and a little spice it becomes dark and crunchy and looks like chunks of coal. And of course, smoky eggplant and grilled meat isn't complete without some bread to mop it up with.

Combine the milk, yeast and 75 ml (2¼ fl oz) of lukewarm water in the bowl of an electric stand mixer. Attach the dough hook and mix at a moderate speed until the yeast has dissolved. Add the flours, salt and vegetable powder and knead for 3–6 minutes until smooth. Cover with a tea towel (dish towel) and leave to rest in a warm place for 45–60 minutes until doubled in size.

Sprinkle some flour on your work surface. Separate the dough into 2 portions and use a rolling pin to roll them into your desired loaf shapes. Allow to prove in a warm spot again for 30 minutes.

Preheat the oven to 200°C (400°F/Gas 6).

Place the bread on two trays and bake for 15–20 minutes until cooked. You can tell if the bread is ready by tapping the base. If it sounds hollow, the bread is cooked.

**Notes** This bread freezes really well and can be used to make burger buns and other bread shapes—a real eye catcher at those special events.

Black vegetable powder can be found at specialty food stores and online. You can also make the bread without it—it will still be delicious.

100 ml (3½ fl oz) milk, at room temperature
1 teaspoon fresh yeast
100 g (3½ oz/⅔ cup) plain (all-purpose) flour, plus extra for dusting
150 g (5½ oz/1 cup) strong flour
pinch of salt flakes
2 tablespoons black vegetable powder (see note)

# VINE LEAF-WRAPPED QUAIL, SUCUK AND CANDIED WALNUTS AND FIGS

Travelling through the bazaars in Turkey can be an overwhelming experience—so much to see, so much to buy and so many new flavours and textures to experience. One product I found in the bazaars was candied walnuts, and I couldn't wait to use them.

Wrapping foods in vine leaves is a popular Middle Eastern technique to hold in the natural juices in a dish. This is a great recipe to make your own—really easy and very tasty.

Put the rice in a small saucepan with enough water to cover by 1 cm (½ inch). Bring to the boil, cover with a lid and cook for 12–15 minutes until the water is absorbed and the rice is plump and tender. Preheat the oven to 250°C (500°F/ Gas 9).

Remove the casing from 500 g (1 lb 2 oz) of the sucuk, set aside the remaining sucuk. Put the sucuk mince, rice, chopped rosemary and parsley stems in a bowl and mix until well combined. Divide into 6 even-sized balls. Mould the quail around the sucuk mixture balls and then wrap in vine leaves. Thread two skewers into each end of the quails and place on a baking tray.

Bake for 8–10 minutes until golden. Remove from the oven and set aside, lightly covered, to rest.

Meanwhile, dice the remaining 100 g (3½ oz) of sucuk and place in a saucepan over medium–high heat. Sauté for a few minutes until crispy, then add the rosemary lengths and toss through until aromatic. Add the figs and walnuts with a generous drizzle of the syrups, bring to the boil, then remove from the heat.

Remove the skewers from the quail and cut the quail in half. Place on serving plates, spoon over the walnut, fig and sucuk garnish, top with rosemary and serve.

**Note** Candied figs and candied walnuts are available at specialist Middle Eastern grocery shops. They can also be purchased online.

65 g (2¼ oz) baldo rice (or arborio rice)

600 g (1 lb 5 oz) sucuk sausages*

1 tablespoon chopped rosemary leaves

handful flat-leaf (Italian) parsley, leaves picked, stems chopped

6 jumbo quails (about 175 g/6 oz each), backbone removed, wings and drumstick intact

16 vine leaves

1 rosemary sprig, broken into 6 lengths

6 candied figs, with syrup (see note)

6 candied walnuts, with syrup (see note)

Cappadocia, Turkey

Preparation time: 25 minutes • Cooking time: 35 minutes • Serves: 6

# WILD GREENS WITH SUCUK BALLS AND EGGS

This is a great dish to share with the family. Just serve it with a bowl of yoghurt and some crusty bread for breakfast, lunch or dinner. You can use other leaves in this dish, besides chicory and silverbeet. Black cabbage or even some Asian greens would work well.

Combine all the sucuk ball ingredients in a bowl. Season generously with salt and pepper. Add 1 tablespoon of water and mix thoroughly until well combined. Roll into about 60 balls and set aside.

Preheat the oven to 200°C (400°F/Gas 6).

Blanch the chicory and silverbeet leaves in a saucepan of boiling salted water over medium–high heat for 5 minutes. Drain and set aside.

Meanwhile, heat 1 tablespoon of the olive oil in a large frying pan over medium–high heat. Add the sucuk balls, in batches, and sauté for a few minutes until evenly browned and caramelised, adding more oil as required. Transfer onto paper towel to absorb any excess oil. Add the onions and garlic to the pan and cook for a few minutes until golden, then add the butter and allow to foam. Add the chicory and silverbeet stems, then add the blanched leaves. Season with the Aleppo pepper, then transfer, with the sucuk balls, into a shallow baking dish. Crack the eggs straight into the dish and bake in the oven for 3–5 minutes or until the egg whites are cooked and the yolk is still a little runny.

Serve immediately, straight from the dish, with yoghurt and crusty bread.

## Sucuk balls
1 kg (2 lb 4 oz) coarsely minced (ground) beef
250 g (9 oz) coarsely minced (ground) lamb tail fat*
3 garlic cloves
2½ tablespoons sweet paprika
1 tablespoon ground cumin

6 chicory stems, leaves picked, stems roughly chopped
6 silverbeet (Swiss chard), leaves separated, stems roughly chopped
80 ml (2½ fl oz/⅓ cup) olive oil
2 brown onions, thinly sliced
4 garlic cloves, crushed
2 tablespoons butter
1 tablespoon red Aleppo pepper* (pul biber)
6 eggs
Greek-style yoghurt and crusty bread, to serve

# BRAISED LAMB WITH SALTBUSH AND ROCKMELON

This is a dish that you are going to want to cook over and over. Dead simple and packed full of flavour. For me a slow-roasted lamb shoulder is one of the best meat dishes you can cook—full of flavour, moisture and so satisfying to eat and serve to your friends and family. Long and slow is the way to go with this recipe. All the work is in the preparation of the meat and then it's just a matter of putting it in the oven and letting it go to work.

If you can't get the saltbush don't worry. It adds real mineral earth saltiness to the dish, but you can make do without it. The real surprise in this dish is the caramelised rockmelon. The sweetness in the dish is a real knockout especially with the introduction of fresh herbs, Aleppo pepper and lemon juice.

Place the lamb in a large wide-based saucepan over high heat and cook, turning occasionally to brown, for 10 minutes. Add the garlic, exposed sides down, onion and spices and continue to cook for 5 minutes until the lamb is evenly sealed and the onion is caramelised. Add the saltbush, if using, and enough stock to cover. Bring to the boil, then reduce the heat to a simmer. Cover with a lid and braise for 3–4 hours or until the meat falls off the bone.

Remove the bone from the lamb and discard. Set the meat aside and keep warm. Increase the heat to high and continue to cook the braising liquid for about 20 minutes until reduced by half. Remove about 125 ml (4 fl oz/½ cup) of the sauce and set aside. Return the lamb to the pan.

Meanwhile, remove the skin from the melon, remove the seeds and cut the flesh into 2 cm (¾ inch) pieces. Place the melon in a frying pan over high heat and caramelise for a few minutes, tossing to cook on all sides (see note). Add the raisins, pine nuts, coriander, mint and lemon zest. Mix until combined and add the reserved sauce to help bind the rockmelon and garnishes together.

Serve the lamb with the melon salad.

**Notes** Saltbush is an edible shrub found in dry inland Australia. It has a pleasant salty flavour. It is available from specialty food suppliers.

The pan has to be really hot to caramelise the melon, otherwise it will stew in its juices.

1 lamb shoulder (about 1.1 kg/ 2 lb 7 oz), bone in
1 garlic bulb, halved crossways
2 brown onions, roughly chopped
1 tablespoon ground cumin
1 tablespoon ground coriander
1 tablespoon red Aleppo pepper* (pul biber)
2 large handfuls saltbush (optional)
2–3 litres (70–105 fl oz/8–12 cups) lamb stock (or another meat stock)
½ rockmelon
85 g (3 oz/½ cup) raisins
235 g (8½ oz/1½ cups) pine nuts, toasted
handful coriander (cilantro), leaves picked and chopped
handful mint, leaves picked and chopped
zest of 1 lemon

# WAGYU BEEF MANTI WITH PEAS, PICKLED ONIONS AND GARLIC YOGHURT

It's the eternal debate—who invented pasta? Well, all I know is that the Turkish 'pasta', manti, is a damn tasty version. While I was in Kayseri I had the pleasure of learning how to make the tiniest little manti I have ever seen. The ladies who taught me told me that the true test of good manti is to be able to fit 40 pieces on each spoon! Well, there is no way I could ever make them that small with my fat fingers, or as tasty as they did, but the version below is a pretty good try.

Mix the manti dough ingredients together with 125 ml (4 fl oz/ ½ cup) of water in the bowl of an electric stand mixer. Using the dough hook attachment, knead at a low speed for 3–6 minutes until a smooth ball is formed. Cover with a tea towel (dish towel) and leave to rest for 30 minutes.

Combine all the wagyu beef filling ingredients in a bowl.

Sprinkle some flour on your work surface and on a tray. Flatten the dough with a rolling pin until 2 mm (1/16 inch) thick. Cut the dough into 1.5 cm (5/8 inch) squares. Place a tiny amount of wagyu mince in the middle of each piece of dough, then bring up all 4 edges to make a diamond shape. Pinch the edges to seal them shut. Repeat this process until all the filling has been used. Place the dumplings on the floured tray (see note).

Combine the garlic yoghurt ingredients in a bowl, cover with plastic wrap and refrigerate until required.

Bring a saucepan of salted water to the boil over high heat. Add the manti and blanch for 2–4 minutes or until they start to float on the surface.

Melt the butter in a large frying pan over medium–high heat. Add the diced sucuk and sauté for a few minutes. Add the peas and baby pickled cocktail onions, and stir through. Add the manti, but don't discard the blanching water.

Put the capsicum paste in a bowl, add a ladleful of the manti blanching water and stir rigorously. Add this to the frying pan and allow to boil for 2 minutes.

Divide the dumplings between four serving bowls. Top with some garlic yoghurt and mint leaves, sprinkle over some Aleppo pepper and serve.

**Notes** Get the kids involved in making these, as small hands are good for this job. They're fiddly, so make a large batch and freeze the excess. These can be frozen if you want to prep them ahead of time, just freeze on a floured tray. When frozen, you can place in freezer bags.

## Manti dough
250 g (9 oz/1⅔ cup) strong flour, plus extra for dusting
1 egg
pinch of salt flakes

## Wagyu beef filling
100 g (3½ oz) minced (ground) wagyu beef
1 garlic clove, crushed
pinch of red Aleppo pepper* (pul biber)

## Garlic yoghurt
200 g (7 oz/¾ cup) Greek-style yoghurt
1 garlic clove, crushed
pinch of salt flakes

1 tablespoon butter
100 g (3½ oz) sucuk sausages*, diced
100 g (3½ oz/⅔ cup) fresh peas
100 g (3½ oz) pickled baby onions
2 tablespoons capsicum paste*
10 mint leaves, torn
pinch of red Aleppo pepper* (pul biber)

Preparation time: 1 hour • Cooking time: 15 minutes • Serves: 4

# ROAST CHICKPEA HUMMUS WITH LAMB KEBAB

On the south-eastern border of Turkey lies the town of Mardin—a lonely forgotten plot of land many people claim as home. There is a huge Syrian community and influence in this part of Turkey, so much so that the food and the language is different from the rest of the country. One night after the cameras were switched off and it was time for dinner I wandered into a little Syrian/Turkish restaurant. They brought out an array of meze and I was blown away by this roast chickpea hummus—so nutty, so texturally different from any hummus I had ever had before. I had to cook it and share it with you.

To make the roast chickpea hummus, combine the chickpeas, garlic, tahini, lemon juice, olive oil, salt and 200 ml (7 fl oz) of warm water in a food processor and blend until smooth. Transfer into a bowl, cover with plastic wrap and refrigerate until required.

Combine the red onion salad ingredients together in a bowl.

Preheat a barbecue grill or hotplate to medium–high.

To prepare the kebabs, thread an onion half onto the end of a skewer. Add 2 pieces of lamb leg, then a piece of fat, and end with another onion half. Repeat to make 8 skewers. Place the skewers on the grill and cook for 3–4 minutes on each side until evenly browned.

Serve the lamb kebabs with the roast chickpea hummus, red onion salad, flat breads and garlic yoghurt.

**Note** Roasting chickpeas gives a beautiful nutty flavour. Because this recipe uses dried chickpeas they require more water than a traditional hummus recipe. They are available at specialist Middle Eastern grocery shops. They can also be purchased online. Alternatively, you can deep fry or roast chickpeas at 180°C (350°F/Gas 4) for about 30 minutes until crisp.

### Roast chickpea hummus
250 g (9 oz) roasted dried chickpeas, plus extra to serve (see note)
2 garlic cloves, peeled
2 tablespoons tahini*
80 ml (2½ fl oz/⅓ cup) lemon juice
splash of olive oil
pinch of salt flakes

### Red onion salad
1 small red onion, thinly shaved
handful flat-leaf (Italian) parsley, leaves picked and torn
handful mint, leaves picked and torn
pinch of sumac*

### Lamb kebabs
8 pickling baby onions, halved crossways
500 g (1 lb 2 oz) deboned lamb leg, diced
200 g (7 oz) lamb tail fat*, finely diced

flat breads, to serve
garlic yoghurt (see page 136), to serve

# ICLI KOFTE WITH GARLIC YOGHURT AND BURNT BUTTER

I've eaten so many versions of this dish in different parts of the world and everyone claims it as their own, but the one we had in Mardin in south-eastern Turkey was right up there with the best of them.

Bring 700 ml (24 fl oz) of water to the boil in a saucepan over high heat. Combine the burghul, sabaht baharat and salt in the bowl of an electric stand mixer. Pour in the boiling water, cover with a lid and stand for 30 minutes.

Attach the dough hook to the mixer and knead the burghul mixture at moderate–high speed for 10–15 minutes, scraping down the sides of the bowl, until the contents resemble a dough consistency—you may need to add a little more hot water if you feel it isn't coming together (see note).

Meanwhile, to make the filling, heat the olive oil in a frying pan over medium heat. Add the lamb and cook for a few minutes, breaking it up with the back of a wooden spoon. Add the onion and stir continuously until the onion is softened. Add the Aleppo pepper and the pistachios. Increase the heat to medium–high and sauté until the onion is translucent and the lamb is evenly browned. Turn out onto a tray and leave to cool.

To make the garlic yoghurt, put the yoghurt and garlic in a bowl. Add the salt and stir through. Cover with plastic wrap and refrigerate until required.

To make the kofte, put a golf ball–sized amount of the burghul mixture in your hand and form into a ball. Poke a hole in the ball with your finger and then make a space for the filling with a tablespoon. Add a teaspoon of the lamb filling and pinch the top to seal the ball. Repeat with the remaining burghul and filling mixtures to make about 20 balls.

Bring a saucepan of water to a simmer over medium–high heat. Add the kofte and cook for 3–4 minutes until cooked. Remove with a slotted spoon.

Meanwhile, melt the butter in a frying pan over medium–high heat until it starts to foam. Add the capsicum paste, Aleppo pepper and pistachios and stir through. Add the lemon juice and stir to combine. Remove from the heat.

Smear some garlic yoghurt on the bottom of each serving plate. Add the icli kofte, spoon over some burnt butter, scatter over the sorrel leaves, if using, and serve immediately.

**Note** It is important to knead the burghul while it's still warm, as this helps it come together.

## Burghul dough

500 g (1 lb 2 oz) fine dark burghul (bulgur)
1 tablespoon sabaht baharat* (Lebanese 7 spice)
pinch of salt flakes

## Lamb and onion filling

1 tablespoon olive oil
200 g (7 oz) minced (ground) lamb
1 brown onion, finely diced
1 tablespoon black Aleppo pepper* (pul biber)
2 tablespoons slivered pistachio nuts

## Garlic yoghurt

260 g (9¼ oz/1 cup) Greek-style yoghurt
2 garlic cloves, crushed
pinch of salt flakes

## Burnt butter

2 tablespoons butter
1 tablespoons capsicum paste*
1 tablespoon red Aleppo pepper* (pul biber)
1 tablespoon pistachio nuts
squeeze of lemon juice

sorrel leaves, to serve (optional)

Cappadocia, Turkey

# CORNBREAD AND FENNEL SEED CRUMBED SARDINES

Sardines are a HUGE part of the Turkish diet. Every village has a specialty or secret way of cooking them. Street-side vendors and corner shops all spruik them to passing potential customers. Cornbread is another item that's hot property in Turkey, especially in the Black Sea regions where there are as many different styles of cornbread as there are sardine dishes.

This dish is an awesome way of bringing them both together and the cornbread has a great way of mellowing out the sometimes overpowering sardine flavour. So for all you sardine haters out there, give this recipe a go. I promise it won't disappoint!

Combine the crumbled cornbread with the polenta, sumac, walnuts, fennel seeds, Aleppo pepper and thyme leaves on a tray.

Place the sardine fillets in the flour, dip in the beaten egg, then place in the cornbread mixture. Press as much as you can into the sardines to enhance the flavour.

Heat the olive oil and butter in a frying pan over medium heat. Carefully place the sardines in the pan, a few at a time, and cook for 1–2 minutes on each side until golden brown. Transfer onto paper towel to soak up the excess oil.

Smear each plate with some garlic yoghurt. Place 3 sardines on top, add the sorrel leaves, if using, and lime, and serve.

**Notes** If you choose to make the cornbread recipe on page 150 it makes more than you need here, but it's handy to have on hand and freezes well. Coarsely crumble and store in ziplock bags in the freezer for up to 3 months.

You can use whiting or prawns instead of sardines.

50 g (1¾ oz/1 cup) crumbled store-bought cornbread (or to make your own, see page 150—see note)
1 tablespoon polenta
1 teaspoon sumac*
30 g (1 oz/¼ cup) walnuts, coarsely crushed
1 teaspoon fennel seeds
1 teaspoon red Aleppo pepper* (pul biber)
6 thyme stems, leaves picked
12 sardine fillets (about 150 g/ 5½ oz each), cleaned (see note)
plain (all-purpose) flour, for dusting
2 eggs, beaten
1 tablespoon olive oil
2 tablespoons butter
garlic yoghurt (see page 140)
sorrel leaves, to serve (optional)
lime cheeks, to serve

Preparation time: 45 minutes • Cooking time: 45 minutes • Serves: 4

# SARDINE AND PRESERVED ORANGE RICE PILAF WITH HERBED CRÈME FRAÎCHE

This is a classic Black Sea dish. Every year when sardines are at their peak, every household and local restaurant is cooking sardine pilaf. Of course, everyone seems to have their own version, and no matter who I spoke to their mum's version was the best. This is my version, which is very close to the traditional dish. I have just tried to make it look a little sharper and the introduction of the preserved orange in the rice adds a nice surprise.

Put the rice in a small saucepan with enough water to cover by 1 cm (½ inch). Bring to the boil, cover with a lid and cook for 10 minutes until the water has been absorbed and the rice is plump, but still slightly firm.

Heat the olive oil in a frying pan over medium heat. Add the pine nuts and stir until coloured, then add the currants, preserved orange and sabaht baharat. Add the rice and toss through, then add the butter, stir through and remove from the heat. Set aside to cool. Add the dill.

Preheat the oven to 170°C (325°F/Gas 3).

Line a 15 cm (6 in) heavy-based ovenproof saucepan or copper pan with baking paper. Arrange the sardine fillets, with the skin side of the sardine facing out, around the side of the pan. Fill the pan with the rice mixture, packing tightly, but stopping about 5 mm (¼ inch) from the top of the pan. Fold over the sardines and place a few more on top to cover the filling. Place a sheet of baking paper over the sardines and then place a weight on top. Bake in the oven for 30 minutes or until firm.

Meanwhile, to make the herbed crème fraîche, place the herbs, lemon zest and olive oil in a food processor and purée until smooth.

Add half the crème fraîche and blend until combined. Transfer to a bowl and fold through the remaining crème fraîche.

Remove the pilaf from the oven and leave to rest for a few minutes, then turn out onto a plate. Dollop a spoonful of the herbed crème fraîche on top and scatter with sorrel leaves, if using. Serve immediately.

**Note** You can still make this dish even if you don't want to create a mould. Simply grill or pan-fry the sardines and serve alongside the rice mixture. In this case, make sure the rice is cooked for a few more minutes until tender.

110 g (3¾ oz/½ cup) baldo rice (or arborio rice)
2 tablespoons olive oil
40 g (1½ oz/¼ cup) pine nuts
2 tablespoons dried currants
2 tablespoons preserved orange*, peel only, diced
1 tablespoon sabaht baharat* (Lebanese 7 spice)
125 g (4½ oz) butter
10 dill sprigs, chopped
500 g (1 lb 2 oz) sardines, filleted and cleaned
sorrel leaves, to serve (optional)

### Herbed crème fraîche

small handful flat-leaf (Italian) parsley
small handful coriander (cilantro)
small handful mint
small handful dill
zest of 1 lemon
60 ml (2 fl oz/¼ cup) olive oil
260 g (9¼ oz/1 cup) crème fraîche

# CHICKEN CORNBREAD DUMPLING SOUP

Another knockout recipe that was taught to me during my travels through Turkey, this one from an old lady who has been cooking the dish for longer than I've been alive. Not much had to be changed— just a little polish here and there—but the addition of the dumpling really brought the dish to a new level. This has become a staple in the Delia household. My kids love it, and it's so simple to make. The polenta gives the dish a lovely toasted flavour, which to me is the thing that makes it special.

180 g (6½ oz) crumbled store-bought cornbread (or to make your own, see page 150)
180 g (6½ oz) minced (ground) chicken (see note)
1 egg white
handful flat-leaf (Italian) parsley, leaves picked and finely chopped
pinch of red Aleppo pepper* (pul biber)
pinch of salt flakes
100 g (3½ oz) butter
1 brown onion, finely diced
1 corn cob, kernels only
2½ tablespoons tomato paste (concentrated purée)
200 g (7 oz) tinned cannellini beans, rinsed and drained
100 g (3½ oz) fine polenta (see note)
80 ml (2½ fl oz/⅓ cup) lemon juice
1 black cabbage (cavolo nero), stems removed
1 tablespoon olive oil
40 g (1½ oz/¼ cup) roasted, peeled hazelnuts, coarsely crushed
1 tablespoon red Aleppo pepper* (pul biber)
zest of 1 lemon

Combine the cornbread, chicken mince, egg white, parsley, Aleppo pepper and salt in the bowl of an electric stand mixer. Attach the paddle attachment and mix until combined, then roll the mixture into walnut-sized balls.

Bring a large saucepan of water to a simmer over medium–high heat. Add the dumplings and cook for 3–5 minutes until firm and cooked through. Remove the dumplings from the pan with a slotted spoon and set aside.

Melt 2 tablespoons of the butter in a large saucepan over medium–high heat. Add the onion and corn and sauté until translucent. Add the tomato paste, beans and polenta, and mix well. Add 2 litres (70 fl oz/8 cups) of water, reduce the heat to low and simmer for 20–25 minutes, stirring occasionally. Add the lemon juice and black cabbage, and season to taste.

Heat the olive oil and remaining butter in a frying pan over medium heat. When the butter starts to foam, add the hazelnuts. Stir through and add the poached dumplings. Add the Aleppo pepper and lemon zest and toss to coat.

Divide the soup between four serving bowls. Add the hazelnut and dumpling mixture and serve immediately.

**Notes** The polenta is used to thicken the soup, but you can leave this out for a different option.

Use other minced meat to change the flavours.

# TEA-SMOKED DUCK WITH BLACK CABBAGE AND HAZELNUT SALAD

This dish sums up the Black Sea region of Turkey for me. Green rolling hills, lots of tea and hazelnuts and game birds.

You'll need a smoking box and a barbecue to really develop the smoky tea flavour in this recipe.

### TURKISH TEA-SMOKED DUCK

Break the hazelnut shells using a mortar and pestle, enough to take out the nut as whole as possible. Place the shells in a smoking box with the tea leaves and place the unpeeled hazelnuts on a baking tray.

Preheat the oven to 180°C (350°F/Gas 4).

Roast the hazelnuts for 8 minutes, peel off the skins and discard, then coarsely crush the hazelnuts and reserve for the black cabbage salad.

Preheat the barbecue to medium–high.

Place the smoking box on the stove, on the highest naked flame. After a couple of minutes it should start smoking. Place the smoking box on the barbecue grill, put a resting rack on top with the duck breasts on it, cover with a lid and leave for 20 minutes.

Remove the duck from the smoker. Heat the butter in a frying pan over medium heat, add the duck and cook for 3 minutes, skin side down, to render the fat. Turn the duck over and cook for a further 3 minutes or until golden. Transfer to a baking tray and finish in the oven for 4 minutes. Set aside to rest for 5–10 minutes before carving. Slice each breast into thin slices.

### CORNBREAD

Preheat the oven to 160°C (315°F/Gas 2–3). Line a 30 x 20 cm (12 x 8 inch) baking tin with baking paper.

Using an electric stand mixer fitted with the whisk attachment, beat the yoghurt, olive oil, eggs and 400 ml (14 fl oz) of water until well combined. Add the flour, baking powder, sugar and salt, and mix on low speed until just combined. With the motor running, slowly add the polenta and mix until smooth—the batter will be quite wet. Pour the mixture into the tin and bake for 20 minutes or until a skewer inserted into the centre comes out clean. Set aside to cool.

### Turkish tea-smoked duck
250 g (9 oz) hazelnuts in shell
80 g (2¾ oz) Turkish tea leaves
(or other black tea leaves)
2 x 200 g (1 lb 2 oz) duck breasts,
skin on (see note)
2 tablespoons butter

### Cornbread
400 g (14 oz) Greek-style yoghurt
60 ml (2 fl oz/¼ cup) olive oil
3 eggs
180 g (6½ oz) plain (all-purpose) flour
20 g (¾ oz) baking powder
60 g (2¼ oz) sugar
pinch of salt
330 g (11½ oz) polenta
2 tablespoons butter

### Black garlic mayonnaise
100 g (3½ oz) black garlic, peeled
(see note)
3 egg yolks
1 egg
1 tablespoon dijon mustard
1 tablespoon lemon juice
300 ml (10½ fl oz) blended oil (50:50
vegetable oil and olive oil)

## Black cabbage and hazelnut salad

3 large black cabbage (cavolo nero)
   leaves, torn
2 garlic cloves
reserved roasted hazelnuts
   (see previous page)
1 tablespoon red Aleppo pepper*
   (pul biber), plus 1 teaspoon extra
60 g (2 oz) pomegranate molasses*
120 ml (3¾ fl oz) olive oil
1 tablespoon lemon juice
1 French shallot, finely diced
5 basil leaves
1 small handful coriander (cilantro),
   leaves picked

Break the cornbread into small chunks to make croutons. Heat the butter in a frying pan over medium heat. When the butter foams, add the cornbread and pan-fry. Set aside until required.

### BLACK GARLIC MAYONNAISE

Put the black garlic, egg yolks, egg, mustard and lemon juice in a food processor and blend until smooth. With the motor running, slowly trickle in the blended oil and continue blending until you have a smooth mayonnaise. Refrigerate until required.

### BLACK CABBAGE AND HAZELNUT SALAD

Blanch the black cabbage leaves in boiling salted water for 10 seconds, then refresh in iced water. Strain and transfer onto paper towel to drain. Set aside until required.

Put the garlic, hazelnuts and Aleppo pepper in a food processor and blend until well combined. Add the pomegranate molasses, olive oil and lemon juice and blend until smooth.

To complete the salad, toss the blanched black cabbage leaves with the hazelnut purée, French shallot, extra Aleppo pepper, basil and coriander. Season with salt and pepper to taste.

### TO SERVE

Place the salad on a plate, add the sliced duck, dollop on the black garlic mayonnaise in the centre of the plate and top with the cornbread croutons. Serve immediately.

**Note** Black garlic is a type of caramelised garlic. It is available at specialty food stores and online.

Tea-smoked duck with
black cabbage and
hazelnut salad

# MASTIC PUDDING WITH CHOCOLATE SOIL, BLACKBERRY SORBET AND ROSEMARY PEARLS

All the side streets in Turkey were filled with blackberry bushes growing wild, and all down the Aegean Coast was a herb I didn't expect to find in Turkey—rosemary. The rosemary and the blackberry together with the mastic is a great combination in this dish. If it's your first time using mastic, go easy as it can be overpowering and is an acquired taste.

### Rosemary pearls
50 g (1¾ oz) honey
1 rosemary sprig
50 g (1¾ oz) tapioca

### Chocolate soil
125 g (4½ oz) sugar
125 g (4½ oz/1¼ cups) almond meal
75 g (2½ oz/½ cup) plain
  (all-purpose) flour
50 g (1¾ oz) cocoa powder
pinch of salt flakes
3 tablespoons butter, melted

### Mastic pudding
500 ml (17 fl oz/2 cups) milk
60 g (2¼ oz) caster (superfine) sugar
20 g (¾ oz) baldo rice (or arborio rice)
1.5 g (½₀ oz) mastic beads
2½ tablespoons butter
50 g (1¾ oz/⅓ cup) plain
  (all-purpose) flour

### Blackberry sorbet
500 g (1 lb 2 oz) blackberries (fresh
  or frozen, thawed)
3 egg whites
200 g (7 oz) caster (superfine) sugar

### To serve
rosemary flowers, to garnish
  (optional)

## ROSEMARY PEARLS

To infuse the honey, combine it with the rosemary in a frying pan over medium heat and simmer for 2 minutes. Remove from the heat.

Place 600 ml (21 fl oz) of water in a large saucepan and bring to the boil over medium–high heat. Add the tapioca and stir frequently for 14 minutes, until the tapioca is cooked and tender. Strain through a sieve and combine the tapioca with the rosemary-infused honey. Refrigerate overnight, to allow the honey to soak into the tapioca.

## CHOCOLATE SOIL

Combine the dry ingredients in a stainless steel bowl. Stir in the melted butter until the mixture looks mealy.

Preheat the oven to 150°C (300°F/Gas 2). Line a baking tray with baking paper.

Spread the mixture out onto the prepared tray and bake for 15 minutes. Remove from the oven and set aside to cool.

Crumble finely to make the soil and store in a sealed container.

## MASTIC PUDDING

Combine the milk, sugar, rice and mastic beads in a saucepan over medium–low heat. Simmer for 15–20 minutes, stirring frequently, until the rice is *al dente*.

Meanwhile, melt the butter in a small saucepan over medium heat. Add the flour and cook, stirring constantly, for 3 minutes or until thickened.

When the rice is cooked, add the flour and butter mixture and continue to stir until the mixture thickens. Reduce the heat to low and continue to cook until the milk mixture starts to slowly boil, then transfer to the bowl of an electric stand mixer. Attach the paddle attachment and beat at high speed until cold. Pour into four serving bowls and refrigerate until set.

## BLACKBERRY SORBET

Purée the blackberries in a bowl with a hand-held stick blender.

Place the blackberry purée and egg whites in the stand mixer bowl and whisk with a whisk attachment at a moderate speed for 10 minutes or until the mixture doubles in size.

Meanwhile, make a syrup by combining the sugar and 100 ml (3½ fl oz) of water in a saucepan over medium–high heat, and cook for approximately 5 minutes to soft ball stage. To test if the syrup is ready drop a small amount into a shallow bowl of cold water to cool it down. It will form a soft ball. If you have a kitchen thermometer, the syrup will be ready when the temperature reaches 115–118°C (about 240°F).

Decrease the speed of the whisk to low and slowly pour in the syrup. Then whisk at a high speed for 3 minutes and continue to whisk until cold. Transfer to a container and freeze.

## TO SERVE

Remove the mastic pudding from the fridge. Add a tablespoon of the tapioca pearls over the top and add a thin layer of the chocolate soil. Add a scoop of blackberry sorbet in the middle. Garnish with rosemary flowers, if using, and serve immediately.

Note The blackberry sorbet is really easy to make, as you don't need an ice-cream machine. Substitute other berries for a different flavour.

Mastic pudding with chocolate soil, blackberry sorbet and rosemary pearls

Preparation time: 30 minutes • Cooking time: 45 minutes • Serves: 4

# ROSEWATER SUTLAC WITH PISTACHIO CRUMBLE

Rice and milk puddings (called sutlac) are a big part of the Middle Eastern and Turkish menu. I have been eating these for as long as I can remember—some good, some not so good, but none of them have been as good as the one I had in the Pontic Mountains around Trabzon. Such a simple dish of sugar, milk and rice, but when it is cooked with love using only the best ingredients possible it's a recipe for success.

Preheat the oven to 170°C (325°F/Gas 3). Line a baking tray with baking paper.

Using an electric stand mixer with the paddle attachment, cream the butter, sugar and pistachio paste for 5 minutes at a moderate speed until pale. Add the flour and pistachios to the bowl, reduce the speed to low and mix until it just comes together.

Transfer the pistachio mixture onto the prepared tray and spread out into an even layer. Place the tray in the oven and bake for 17 minutes or until golden. Remove the shortbread from the oven and set aside until cool enough to handle. Break up into a crumble.

To make the rosewater sutlac, place the milk in a saucepan over medium–high heat. Simmer until the milk has reduced by a third.

In a separate saucepan, cook the rice, adding the milk, ladle by ladle, and stirring continuously until *al dente*. Add the sugar and rosewater, stir well and then pour into serving bowls.

Place a mound of pistachio crumble on top of the sutlac. Top with pistachios and mint leaves, and serve either hot or cold.

**Notes** Pistachio nut paste is available from specialist Middle Eastern grocery shops. It can also be purchased online.

Use a really fresh cow's or goat's milk for superior flavour.

## Pistachio crumble

160 g butter, at room temperature

75 g (2½ oz/⅓ cup) caster (superfine) sugar

1 tablespoon pistachio nut paste (see note)

250 g (9 oz/1⅔ cups) plain (all-purpose) flour

125 g (4½ oz) pistachio nuts, plus extra to serve

## Rosewater sutlac

1 litre (35 fl oz/4 cups) milk (see note)

60 g (2¼ oz) baldo rice (or arborio rice)

70 g (2½ oz) sugar

125 ml (4 fl oz/½ cup) rosewater

small handful mint leaves, to serve

# PUMPKIN TURKISH DELIGHT

I love the way the ladies I spent time with in the hills surrounding Fethiye made sucuk pekmez—a sweet made by dipping walnuts or pistachios in syrup to create a sausage. Thickening the molasses with semolina made me think about what other fruits or vegetables I could try using the same technique. The sweetness of pumpkin made me think it would be an easy substitute for the pekmez in the form of a purée, and it turned out to be a great dish. The icing sugar snow really made it feel like Turkish delight and also represented the snow-capped mountains around Fethiye.

Peel the candied pumpkin, place in a food processor and blend until smooth.

Heat the candied pumpkin purée, sugar syrup and 300 ml (10½ fl oz) of water in a heavy-based saucepan, whisking occasionally, until the mixture starts to boil. Add the semolina and stir through, then reduce the temperature to medium–low and cook for 5–8 minutes.

Transfer the mixture into the bowl of an electric stand mixer, attach the paddle attachment, and beat at moderate speed, adding the butter a little at a time, for 10 minutes or until completely cool.

Line a tray with baking paper and dust with some of the icing sugar and cornflour. Add the walnuts to the pumpkin mixture and stir through. Pour the mixture onto the sugared tray and flatten it out evenly. Dust the top with icing sugar and cornflour to resemble snow and then refrigerate for 3–4 hours to set.

Portion the pumpkin Turkish delight into 4 cm (1½ inch) squares. Dust with any remaining icing sugar and cornflour and serve.

**Notes** Sugar syrup is available from specialist confectioners' stores. You can also make your own sugar syrup by mixing equal quantities of sugar and water in a saucepan over low heat until the sugar has dissolved.

750 g (1 lb 10 oz) candied spiced pumpkin (winter squash—see page 61)
450 ml (16 fl oz) sugar syrup (see note)
300 g (10½ oz) fine semolina
100 g (3½ oz) butter
150 g (5½ oz) icing (confectioners') sugar
150 g (5½ oz) cornflour (cornstarch)
60 g (2¼ oz/½ cup) walnuts, toasted and roughly chopped

Essaouira

# MOROCCO

Magical and mystical. Overflowing with opulence, and a splash of danger and excitement. These were my childhood ideas of Morocco, which came about by watching old movies about the Crusades, Moorish kings and knights, and Bible epics.

On the silver screen I saw a landscape that was hard and unforgiving, yet it had this mesmerising beauty that transfixed its visitors. I could almost smell the banquets richly perfumed with the flavours that had been discovered along the medieval spice routes and brought back to the kitchens of the kings. Morocco, to me, has always been liberally sprinkled with wonder and enchantment.

Fez. From hidden alleys of the medina that reveal some beautiful secrets like bissara and sweet mint tea, to wondrous bazaars thick with the aromas of tagine, simmering with saffron, to the city's glorious architecture—stunning palaces and riads that have been restored to their former beauty. I've experienced no other place on earth like it. The adrenaline rush you get when you suddenly realise that you are lost in one of the estimated 9000 streets and alleys of the Fez medina is like no other. Many streets don't have a name ... there are no maps and the sun is about to set. You are stuck in an ancient world with no Google or GPS, and filled with a sense of helplessness. To me, that is the most beautiful thing about Fez. You've got no choice but to submit to its ways. You simply have no choice. And then the magic takes hold.

I closed my eyes and started to remember the movies I'd watched as a child. Before I knew it I was seeing caravan traders walking down the streets laden with treasures from their long trek through the desert—huge crest moon–shaped swords, cloths of gold, bright coloured turquoise turbans and jewel-studded sashes. Camels and donkeys bustling through the tight alleys loaded with supplies and riches. Laughter and music echoing from friends and families reunited after returning home from battling in the Crusades.

It's not that I have some wildly imaginative fantasy about living in a time long forgotten, but it's not that hard to envisage such a world in Morocco. The details and situations may have changed, but Fez, in particular, is still the same. Families are still living in the same homes that have stood here for hundreds of years, donkeys still roam the streets carrying goods to the market or hides to the tannery. Street vendors still work the same corners that have been worked for centuries and the call to prayer still bellows through the air from medieval minarets.

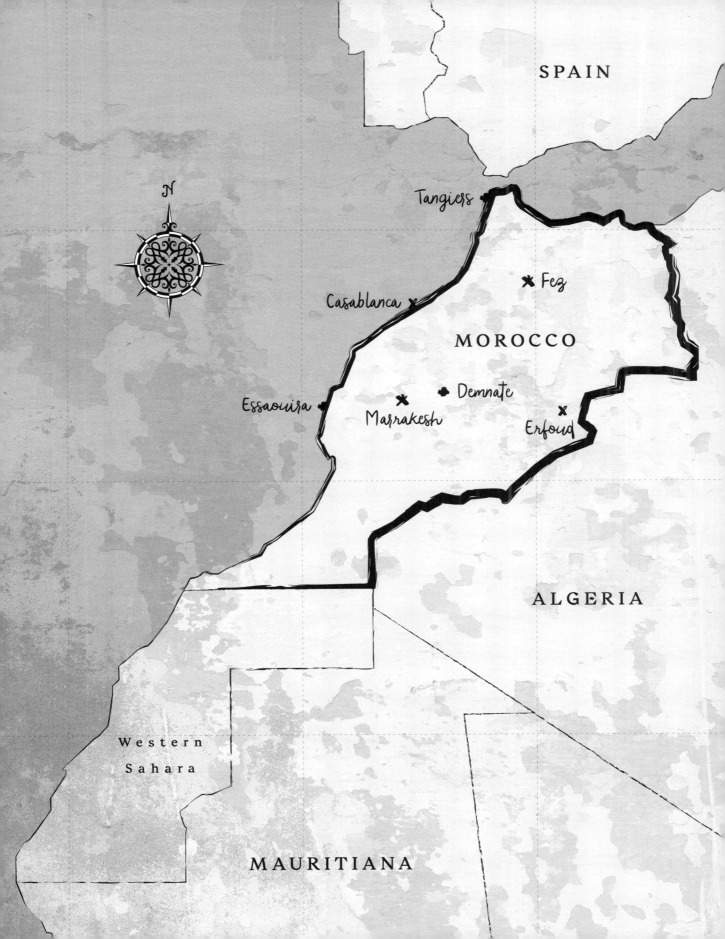

From Fez it was on through freezing snow to Erfoud and Rissani where I met Berber families who showed me the beauty of the desert and a simpler way of life using only what you need, or what the land can provide. Wind-shaped sand dunes seemed to stretch for miles, changing shape right before your eyes with the setting sun. Oases emerged where life seemed non-existent, filled with people who welcomed me with open arms and dishes ready to fill my empty belly. Date and orange fields filled with the sweet scent of honey, roasting almonds and freshly baked breads and pastries, and of course the ubiquitous tagines.

Bright green fields filled with poppies, wild thyme and sunflowers would burst into birdsong with the rising sun. And as I crossed the snow-capped Atlas Mountains into Demnate the land filled with life and new ingredients: preserved lemons and fruits, and fermented butter from the sheep and cows that roam this beautiful and abundant landscape.

BANG, and into the hustle and bustle of Marrakesh, where snake charmers, fortune tellers, meat cooking over coals, and bus-loads of tourists with selfie sticks all cram into the Jemaa el Fna. Forget going to university to get a degree in sales or marketing. The store owners and food vendors here have had thousands of years to perfect their craft and can sell you anything—usually something you would never imagine buying. And if you don't buy it on their first sales pitch they seem to cast a magic spell that ensures you buy it out of guilt. You may as well admit defeat; you have no chance against these masters of persuasion and trickery.

Marrakesh is electric, alive and pumping. It's like watching your favourite band at a live show, drinking until you can't stand, then devouring a greasy burger and chips at 3 am on the way home. A bloody amazing night out, no regrets, but you can't quite remember everything that happened.

Morocco will always be a place that excites me. I love the history in the food and the cities, the excitement and chaos I sense all around when walking the streets. You can either come to Morocco and try to change her into what you want or hope she can be, and fail like countless numbers of ruling factions have done over the centuries. Or, you can immerse yourself in what Morocco is and accept her in all her crazy glory. Revel in her successes and look for beauty where it is not so obvious. The soul of the Moroccan people and their country is pure and beautiful. It may not be what you are used to or what you had expected, but if it were wouldn't you be just a little disappointed? ✸

*Immerse yourself in what Morocco is and accept her in all her crazy glory.*

# BISSARA WITH ROASTED GARLIC OIL, SCALLOPS, CARROTS AND CUMIN

Traditional bissara is a full-on, earthy dish that really sums up the souk. Gutsy and surprising with just enough spice and olive oil to make it special. But to be honest, it's not really everyone's cup of tea. The broad beans in the traditional recipe can be over-pungent, so I have tamed the recipe and introduced some finesse and sweetness, while trying to keep the essence of the dish intact with a subtle use of spice.

Drain the soaked lima beans and set aside.

Shell the broad beans and discard the large pods. Bring a saucepan of water to the boil and blanch the beans for 1 minute in the boiling water. Remove with a slotted spoon and peel off the skin to double pod the beans. Discard the skins. Continue double podding the beans until you have 185 g (6½ oz/1 cup).

Heat the olive oil in a large saucepan over high heat. Add the onion, celery, garlic and spices, and fry for 4–5 minutes until fragrant. Add the lima beans, cover with 1.5 litres (52 fl oz/6 cups) of water and cook for 15 minutes or until the beans are tender. Remove from the heat and purée with a hand-held stick blender until smooth. Adjust the seasoning and set aside.

Heat the sugar, lemon juice and 100 ml (3½ fl oz) of water in a small saucepan over high heat until the sugar has dissolved. Remove from the heat and pour into a large bowl. Cover and refrigerate until cold.

Put the carrots in a saucepan of boiling salted water over high heat and cook for 3 minutes or until just tender. Remove and drain, then refresh in the bowl of cold lemon sugar water (see note). Season and set aside.

Put the broad beans and lentils in a bowl with the coriander leaves and toss to combine.

Heat a little oil in a small frying pan over high heat, add the almonds and scallops and cook, turning, for 30–60 seconds until seared on both sides and just cooked through.

Place the broad beans and lentil salad in four shallow bowls, add the carrots and top with the scallops. Pour over a little lima bean purée and drizzle with harissa. Sprinkle over extra paprika and cumin and serve.

Note Refreshing the carrots in the lemon, sugar and water enhances their natural sweetness. It is a great way to stop the cooking process and retain some texture.

300 g (10½ oz/1½ cups) dried lima beans, soaked overnight

500 g (1 lb 2 oz) fresh broad (fava) beans

1 tablespoons olive oil, plus extra

1 small brown onion, diced

1 celery stalk, diced

2 garlic cloves, crushed

1 teaspoon smoked paprika, plus extra to serve

½ teaspoon dried cumin, plus extra to serve

100 g (3½ oz) sugar

100 ml (3½ fl oz) lemon juice

2 handfuls dutch carrots, scrubbed, ends trimmed

210 g (7½ oz/1 cup) puy lentils, cooked

large handful fresh coriander (cilantro), leaves picked

handful almonds, roughly chopped

500 g (1 lb 2 oz) small scallops, roe removed

harissa*, to serve

# RFISSA

Anytime someone teaches me a dish of celebratory and cultural significance I sit up and listen. There was a lot to love about this dish when I first tried it in Morocco—the use of fenugreek and saffron with lentils and harissa created a beautiful sauce for the chicken to be braised in. This is my spin on it.

Place all the marinade ingredients in a shallow bowl and mix well. Add a few tablespoons of water to make a thick paste. Add the chicken and rub the marinade all over. Cover with plastic wrap and place in the fridge for 2–3 hours.

Meanwhile, soak the fenugreek seeds for 2 hours.

Heat 80 ml (2½ fl oz/⅓ cup) of the olive oil in a large saucepan over medium heat. Add the onions and cook for 10 minutes until well caramelised. Remove and set aside. Add the marinated chicken to the pan and cook for 8–10 minutes, turning occasionally, until browned on all sides. Return the onions to the pan, add the saffron and remaining 185 ml (6 fl oz/¾ cup) of olive oil and 1 litre (35 fl oz/ 4 cups) of water. Add the fenugreek, lentils and chickpeas and bring to the boil, then reduce the heat to a simmer and cook for 40 minutes. Remove from the heat.

Remove the chicken from the pan, place in a bowl and leave until cool enough to handle then shred the meat and discard the bones. Add the coriander and enough cooking sauce to the shredded chicken meat to combine. Reserve half a cup of the remaining sauce for the salad, along with a cupful of chickpeas, lentils and fenugreek in a bowl.

Preheat the oven to 200°C (400°F/Gas 6). Line a baking tray with baking paper.

Lay the pastry into long strands, about 12 x 8 cm (4½ x 3¼ inch) lengths. Brush one side with the melted butter.

Place 3 large tablespoons of the shredded chicken mixture at one end of the pastry and roll up. Repeat to make four long parcels.

Place the pastries on the prepared tray, spoon over the remaining sauce and bake for 30 minutes or until golden.

Add the radish, frisee leaves and eggs to the reserved bowl of sauce, chickpeas, lentils and fenugreek. Toss together and then dress with some harissa.

Remove the kataifi from the oven and transfer onto a serving platter. Drizzle over the reserved sauce and serve with the salad.

Note Kataifi pastry is available at specialty Middle Eastern grocery stores.

**Saffron marinated chicken**
1 teaspoon ground turmeric
3 teaspoons ground ginger
3 garlic cloves, crushed
pinch of saffron powder
2 chicken leg quarters (about
    400 g/14 oz each)

50 g (1¾ oz) fenugreek seeds
265 ml (9½ fl oz) olive oil
4 brown onions, thinly sliced
pinch of saffron threads, toasted
100 g (3½ oz) green lentils
160 g (5½ oz) tinned chickpeas,
    rinsed and drained
handful coriander (cilantro), leaves
    picked and chopped
375 g (13 oz) kataifi pastry (see note)
125 g (4½ oz) butter, melted
1 baby radish, thinly sliced
handful frisee, leaves picked
4 hard-boiled eggs, sliced
harissa*, to serve

# BRAISED CHICKPEA STEW WITH LAMB SHIN, EGGPLANT AND GRAINS

It's the little things I pick up when I'm on my spice journey that really stick with me. The technique of putting pulses in a muslin bag and cooking it with meat stock was a revelation I discovered in Morocco. It made perfect sense, but I had never seen it before. This way I could cook all my grains and pulses together and they could soak up all the flavour of the dish without being dispersed all through it. Genius!

Soak the chickpeas in cold water for 12 hours or overnight.

Combine the saffron with 750 ml (26 fl oz/3 cups) of boiling water.

Preheat the oven to 165°C (320°F/Gas 2–3).

Mix the remaining spices together in a bowl and season with salt and freshly ground black pepper. Rub the mixture onto the lamb.

Heat the olive oil in a large flameproof casserole dish or tagine dish over medium heat. Add the lamb and brown on all sides. Add the onions, carrots and half the dates, then add the tomatoes and saffron water.

Put the soaked chickpeas in a muslin (cheesecloth) bag, leaving some room for them to expand. Put the freekeh, rice and burghul in a second muslin bag, leaving room for expansion in this bag, too. Gently place these in the dish.

Cover the dish with a lid or foil, place in the oven and cook for 2½ hours or until the meat is tender and falling off the bones.

Meanwhile, place the whole eggplant over a gas flame or barbecue grill and cook until the skin is charred and the eggplant is soft. Set aside to cool, then remove the skin and cut the flesh into rough chunks. Set aside.

Make some confit garlic by heating the garlic cloves with enough olive oil to cover, in a saucepan over medium heat for 30 minutes or until they are soft and caramelised. Set aside.

Remove the casserole from the oven. Remove the muslin bags and carefully place the contents in a large mixing bowl. Add the eggplant and remaining dates. Season with salt and pepper. Add the parsley and coriander.

Gently pull the lamb meat from the bones in large chunks. Put the meat into a frying pan with the cooked onions and a ladleful of juices from the casserole dish. Bring to the boil, then add the confit garlic cloves. Season with salt and lemon zest. Add some harissa to taste.

Place the grains in a serving dish, gently spoon over the meat and serve.

200 g (7 oz/1 cup) dried chickpeas
1 teaspoon saffron powder
2 teaspoons ground turmeric
2 teaspoons smoked paprika
1 tablespoon ground cumin
1 kg (2 lb 4 oz) lamb shin (osso buco)
60 ml (2 fl oz/¼ cup) olive oil
10 pickling onions, peeled
2 carrots, peeled and cut into
    large chunks
10 medjool dates, pitted
4 large ripe tomatoes, grated
150 g (5½ oz/1 cup) freekeh
220 g (7¾ oz/1 cup) rice
45 g (1½ oz/¼ cup) burghul (bulgur)
1 large eggplant (aubergine)
8 garlic cloves, unpeeled
small handful coriander (cilantro),
    leaves picked and chopped
small handful flat-leaf (Italian)
    parsley, leaves picked and
    chopped
zest of 1 lemon
harissa*, to serve

Preparation time: 20 minutes • Cooking time: 2 hours • Serves: 8

# FOOT OF THE MOUNTAIN COUSCOUS WITH GARDEN VEGETABLES

I remember eating couscous dishes all over Morocco. Lots of flavour and such attention to detail in the presentation of each dish. But for me the biggest let-down was the way it was prepared. The vegetables were always overcooked and collapsed into one. My version pays homage to the beautiful produce I found as I crossed the Atlas Mountains where the foot of the mountain opened up in full bloom and the air was filled with the smell of wild thyme.

To make the vegetable stock, place all the ingredients and 2 litres (70 fl oz/ 8 cups) of water in a large stockpot over high heat and bring to the boil, then reduce the heat to a simmer and cook for 2 hours. Season with salt and pepper, strain and set aside.

Preheat the oven to 200°C (400°F/Gas 6).

Place all the vegetables in a large roasting tin and toss with the olive oil. Add the garlic and rosemary. Cook for about 1½ hours until tender and caramelised.

Meanwhile, blend the thyme and butter together in a small bowl with a wooden spoon, season with salt and pepper and set aside.

Heat the stock in a saucepan over high heat and add a pinch of saffron threads.

To make the mountain couscous, first rub 1 tablespoon of oil into the couscous to prevent lumps. Transfer into a large bowl with double the quantity of hot stock and the salt. Set aside and allow to absorb the liquid completely. Set aside the remaining stock. Add the lemon zest, preserved lemon, almonds and fresh herbs to the couscous. Rub some of the thyme butter through the couscous to make it fluffy and aerated.

Reheat the remaining stock, with harissa to taste, then pour into a large serving jug (pitcher).

Put the vegetables on a large serving plate and drizzle over some of the harissa stock and the remaining thyme butter. Scatter over the fennel fronds and serve with the remaining sauce and the couscous.

## Vegetable stock
2 large fennel bulbs, halved
2 large brown onions, halved
2 leeks, trimmed and halved
4 large tomatoes, halved
large pinch of saffron threads
handful herbs (such as rosemary, bay leaf, thyme)

3 small onions
3 small zucchini (courgettes) (or zucchini flowers), cut lengthways
900 g (2 lb) kent pumpkin (winter squash), cut into thin wedges
2 small fennel bulbs, halved, fronds reserved
½ small cabbage, quartered
8 mixed new potatoes
8 purple potatoes (optional)
8 mixed dutch carrots, scrubbed
125 ml (4 fl oz/½ cup) olive oil, plus 1 tablespoon extra for the couscous
6 garlic cloves
4 rosemary sprigs
handful fresh thyme, leaves picked
125 g (4½ oz) butter, softened
pinch of saffron threads
500 g (1 lb 2 oz) couscous
pinch of salt
zest of 1 lemon
1 tablespoon chopped preserved lemon peel
95 g (3¼ oz) chopped almonds, toasted
handful fresh herbs (such as coriander/cilantro, mint), chopped
2 tablespoons harissa*

Preparation time: 30 minutes • Cooking time: 40 minutes • Serves: 4–6

# SARDINE KEFTA WITH FRESH CHERMOULA SALAD

If sardines aren't really your thing (I get it that they can be a bit full on), that doesn't mean you should just black-list them for the rest of your days. They are a great little fish, sustainable as hell and have a great flavour. The flavour intensity just needs to be turned down from a 10 to a 3, and this recipe does just that. The introduction of carrot, adding heaps of sweetness, and some choice spicing really mellows out the fishy sardine flavour. This is a really easy and safe way to start back on the sardine dating scene. Come on. Give it a go.

Mix the sardines and fish with the diced garlic, breadcrumbs, chilli, mint, spices, parsley and lemon zest to bind. Roll into golf ball–sized balls and set aside.

Heat the olive oil in a flameproof tagine dish or casserole dish over medium heat. Place the kefta in the tagine and brown for a few minutes on all sides, turning as required. Remove the kefta from the tagine and set aside. Place the banana shallots and garlic slices in the tagine and cook over low heat for a few minutes until golden and softened.

Place the remaining ingredients in the tagine along with the kefta. Pour over enough saffron water to cover. Place over a gentle heat, cover with a lid and cook for about 20 minutes, until the sauce has thickened and the kefta are cooked through.

To make the chermoula paste, blend all the ingredients together in a food processor until smooth. Store in an airtight container in the fridge until ready to use.

To make the salad, mix the herbs and olive oil through the chermoula in a serving bowl.

Serve the tagine in the middle of the table for people to help themselves with pan-fried potato breads (see page 182) and the fresh chermoula salad on the side.

Note Ask your fishmonger to mince the fish. If you're not a fan of sardines, substitute with any white fish as it's really simple and delicious.

Banana shallots are mild, elongated shallots. If you can't find them, use French shallots instead.

Chermoula paste may be stored in the fridge for 2 weeks.

200 g (7 oz) fresh sardine fillets, minced (ground) (see note)
300 g (10½ oz) white fish fillets, minced (ground) (see note)
2 garlic cloves, finely diced
55 g (2 oz/½ cup) dry breadcrumbs
1 red bird's eye chilli, seeded and diced
1 teaspoon dried mint
1 teaspoon ground turmeric
1 teaspoon sweet paprika
small handful flat-leaf (Italian) parsley, leaves picked and chopped
zest of 1 lemon
2 tablespoons olive oil
6 whole banana shallots, peeled and halved (see note)
6 garlic cloves, sliced
2 tomatoes, grated
2 carrots, grated
1 litre (35 fl oz/4 cups) saffron water*

## Chermoula paste
1 garlic bulb
4 French shallots
3 tablespoons coriander seeds
3 tablespoons cumin seeds
1 preserved lemon, peel only
125 ml (4 fl oz/½ cup) olive oil

## Fresh chermoula salad
handful flat-leaf (Italian) parsley, leaves picked
handful coriander (cilantro), leaves picked
handful mint, leaves picked
80 ml (2½ fl oz/⅓ cup) olive oil
1 tablespoon chermoula paste (see above)

# PAN-FRIED POTATO BREADS

**Shut the gates and lock the door, because when people start to smell the aromas when you start cooking these little bundles of joy you will have lines out the front ready to get their serve. I was over-eating either heavy bread or stodgy potato with every dish when I was travelling through Morocco, so it got me thinking—what if I could keep the integrity of the cuisine, but raise the bread up to make it a hero of the dish, not just a sauce mopper or filler? This light, fluffy potato bread was the result.**

Heat the milk and sugar in a small saucepan over low heat until warm. Add the yeast, remove from the heat and allow to sit for 15 minutes.

Meanwhile, put the potatoes in a large saucepan, cover with cold water and bring to the boil over high heat, then cook for 10 minutes or until tender. Drain and pass through a mouli or food mill or sieve until very smooth and then place in a large bowl. Add the eggs, flour and extra virgin olive oil and mix well to combine. Add the yeast mixture and knead well, adding more flour if necessary to keep the batter from becoming too sticky. Cover with a tea towel (dish towel) and set aside in a warm place for 1 hour or until doubled in size. Punch down the dough and divide into 12 portions.

Lightly flour your work surface and roll each piece of dough out to about 2 cm (¾ inch) thickness.

Heat 1 tablespoon of the olive oil in a large heavy-based frying pan over high heat. Working in batches, fry the dough for about 5 minutes until golden brown, turning over halfway through. Remove from the pan and transfer onto a plate lined with paper towel to soak up the excess oil. Repeat with the remaining oil and dough.

**Notes** Make sure the potatoes are cooked all the way through as you don't want any lumps.

You can sprinkle the dough with semolina for extra texture on the flat breads just before cooking in the pan.

This is a versatile bread that goes well with many Moroccan dishes; for example, it's delicious served with the Sardine kefta with fresh chermoula salad on page 181.

125 ml (4 fl oz/½ cup) milk

2 tablespoons sugar

2 teaspoons dried yeast

500 g (1 lb 2 oz) roasting potatoes (such as russet/Idaho or king Edward), peeled and cut into chunks

2 eggs

525 g (1 lb 2½ oz/3½ cups) plain (all-purpose) flour, plus extra for dusting

60 ml (2 fl oz/¼ cup) extra-virgin olive oil

125 ml (4 fl oz/½ cup) olive oil, for frying

The rear wall of El Badi Palace, Marrakesh

# LAMB SHOULDER WITH POTATO AND EGGPLANT TAGINE

You can't beat eating a traditional tagine in the Sahara. Even if the dish isn't the most mind-blowing, the atmosphere of eating under the stars in the desert with Berbers is an experience that is hard to match. Here's my rendition of a traditional Moroccan tagine, without the magical setting admittedly, but packed full of beauty in the flavours of the dish.

Mix together the cumin, paprika and salt in a bowl and then rub generously all over the lamb pieces.

Heat the olive oil in a heavy-based frying pan over high heat, add the lamb and cook for 15 minutes, turning occasionally, until browned on all sides. Remove and set aside.

Add the onions to the pan and sauté until softened and starting to colour. Add the garlic and cook, stirring frequently, for a minute until fragrant. Transfer the onion mixture into a flameproof tagine dish or casserole dish and place a layer of potatoes on top. Add the meat and top with the eggplant wedges. Add the tomatoes.

Dissolve the saffron in 1 litre (35 fl oz/4 cups) of water and then pour into the tagine dish to cover the lamb. Nestle in the dates. Cover with a lid, bring to the boil over high heat, reduce the heat to a simmer and cook for 45 minutes or until the meat is tender.

Meanwhile, make the gremolata. Heat the olive oil and butter in a small frying pan over high heat, add the bread chunks and cook, turning regularly, until the bread is crunchy and browned all over. Remove from the heat, add the walnuts, dates, ginger, parsley and lemon zest and stir together. Check and adjust the seasoning.

Serve the tagine with a generous amount of gremolata over the top and a drizzle of harissa.

3 tablespoons ground cumin
2 tablespoons sweet paprika
1 tablespoon salt
1 kg (2 lb 4 oz) boneless lamb
    shoulder, cubed
2 tablespoons olive oil
2 large brown onions, sliced
6 garlic cloves, crushed
3 potatoes, peeled and sliced
3 Lebanese (long thin) eggplants
    (aubergine), cut into large wedges
2 tomatoes, grated
pinch of saffron threads
6 medjool dates, pitted

### Gremolata

2 tablespoons olive oil
1½ tablespoons butter
a small roll of good quality artisan
    bread, broken into chunks
115 g (4 oz/1 cup) walnuts, toasted
160 g (5½ oz/1 cup) medjool dates,
    pitted and roughly diced
1 tablespoon freshly grated ginger
handful flat-leaf (Italian) parsley,
    chopped
zest of 1 lemon
harissa*, to serve

# HARIRA SOUP WITH PAN-FRIED CHICKEN DUMPLINGS AND BROAD BEAN SALAD

**This was a really hard dish to draw inspiration from. I really love it just the way it is. Hearty, and full of flavour and love. It's a big hug from Mum when you haven't seen her in a while, and how can you get better than that? So I just tried to pick up on the things that made the dish special when I tasted it in Marrakesh, and have tried to bring them to life in a lighter way. The best thing that came out of the recipe is the chicken dumpling—mega tasty and something great to make with the kids.**

Heat the olive oil in a large saucepan over high heat, add the garlic and onions and cook for about 5 minutes to soften without colouring. Add the spices, rice and lentils, stirring to coat, and cook for 2 minutes, then add the tomatoes and 1.25 litres (44 fl oz/5 cups) of water. Season with sea salt and freshly ground black pepper. Bring to the boil then simmer for 40 minutes. Add the parsley, remove from the heat and then purée using a hand-held stick blender until smooth.

To make the dumplings, heat 1 tablespoon of the olive oil in a frying pan over high heat, add the celery, garlic shoots and onion and sauté for 1–2 minutes until softened. Remove from the heat, transfer into a large mixing bowl and set aside to cool.

Add the chives, ginger and chicken mince to the bowl and mix together well. Place a teaspoon of the chicken mixture in the middle of a gyoza wrapper, fold in half, brush the edge with water and pleat the pastry to seal the edge. Repeat with the remaining filling and gyoza.

Heat the remaining oil in a large shallow frying pan over medium heat. Add the gyoza and fry on one side for 5 minutes until the pastry is golden. Reduce the heat to low, add the stock, cover with a lid and steam for about 4 minutes until the liquid has evaporated and the filling is cooked. Remove from the heat and keep warm.

Mix the broad bean salad ingredients together in a small bowl.

To serve, place 3 gyoza in the middle of each serving bowl, pour over some harira and dress the top of the dumplings with some of the broad bean salad. Serve with the remaining broad bean salad.

*Notes* Gyoza wrappers are available from Asian supermarkets.

## Harira soup
2 tablespoons olive oil
2 garlic cloves, chopped
2 large red onions, chopped
1 teaspoon ground turmeric
1 teaspoon ground cumin
1 teaspoon cayenne pepper
pinch of saffron threads
½ teaspoon ground ginger
1 cinnamon stick
110 g (3¾ oz/½ cup) rice
215 g (7½ oz/1 cup) green lentils
400 g (14 oz) tinned diced tomatoes
2 tablespoons chopped flat-leaf
  (Italian) parsley

## Chicken dumplings
60 ml (2 fl oz/¼ cup) olive oil
1 celery stalk, diced
4 garlic shoots
½ brown onion, finely diced
2 tablespoons finely chopped chives
1 tablespoon freshly grated ginger
150 g (5½ oz) minced (ground)
  chicken thigh
24 gyoza pastry rounds (see note)
250 ml (9 fl oz/1 cup) chicken stock

## Broad bean salad
185 g (6½ oz/1 cup) broad (fava)
  beans, double podded
1 preserved lemon, peel only,
  finely diced
2 French shallots, thinly sliced
handful coriander (cilantro), leaves
  picked

# WAGYU BEEF WITH ROASTED CAULIFLOWER HUMMUS AND AMLOU DRESSING

I remember when I was first exposed to argan oil several years ago. I have to say I wasn't too impressed. A lot of Morocco's argan oil is produced in a very primitive way, where the quality of the oil is compromised and a very sub-par product is the end result.

I can't tell you how excited I was to finally experience argan oil at its best. It was a whole new experience and has started me on a journey exploring the flavour possibilities for this truly beautiful product. Be careful to use the right oil.

Preheat the oven to 200°C (400°F/Gas 6). Line a baking tray with baking paper.

Put the cauliflower florets on the prepared tray and roast for 40 minutes or until soft and lightly coloured. Remove from the oven and set aside to cool (see note).

Season the beef with freshly ground black pepper and sea salt. Sear for 10 minutes on all sides in a heavy-based frying pan over high heat. Add the rosemary sprig to the pan and baste the beef with the pan juices. Transfer to the oven and cook for 4 minutes. Remove from the oven and set aside to rest.

Put the cauliflower in a food processor with the cream and blend until smooth. Add the chickpeas, garlic, tahini and lemon juice and blitz until smooth. Check and adjust the seasoning.

To make the amlou dressing, mix together the argan oil, almonds, honey and sherry vinegar in a small bowl.

In a separate bowl, mix the Aleppo pepper, shallots and chives with a couple of spoonfuls of the amlou.

Slice the beef thinly. Toss with some amlou dressing, radishes and the salad leaves.

Place the roasted cauliflower hummus on a plate, top with the wagyu beef and salad, drizzle over any remaining dressing and serve.

Note Roasting the cauliflower brings out the natural sweetness and gives the hummus a delicious flavour.

1 cauliflower head, broken into florets
500 g (1 lb 2 oz) wagyu beef rump
1 rosemary sprig
125 ml (4 fl oz/½ cup) thickened (pouring) cream
200 g (7 oz) tinned chickpeas, rinsed and drained
3 garlic cloves
65 g (2¼ oz/¼ cup) tahini*
2 tablespoons lemon juice
125 ml (4 fl oz/½ cup) argan oil*
160 g (5½ oz/1 cup) almonds, roasted
2 tablespoons honey
60 ml (2 fl oz/¼ cup) sherry vinegar
1 teaspoon black Aleppo pepper* (pul biber)
2 French shallots, diced
1 tablespoon finely chopped chives
small radishes, watercress and sorrel leaves, to serve

Preparation time: 15 minutes • Cooking time: 1 hour 40 minutes • Serves: 8

# VEAL SHIN AND SAFFRON WITH CARROT AND PRESERVED ORANGE PURÉE

This was one of the tastiest dishes I ate while in Morocco—soft meat, big saffron and caramelised onion flavours and that little hint of sweet and salty preserved citrus right at the end. This is a great wintry recipe you will want to sit down to with some good bread, a big bottle of red and some friends or family to help you finish off all the sauce at the bottom of the dish.

Put the veal in a bowl, add the saffron, cumin and 1 tablespoon of the olive oil and combine to completely cover the meat. Season with salt and pepper.

Heat another tablespoon of the oil in a flameproof tagine dish or casserole dish over medium heat, add the veal and cook for a few minutes on each side to brown off. Remove the meat from the pan, add the remaining oil and sauté the onions, garlic and preserved lemon for a few minutes until softened. Deglaze the pan with the wine, then add the stock and bring to the boil. Return the meat to the pan, reduce the heat to low and cook for 1½ hours until the meat falls away from the bones.

Meanwhile, put the carrots, onions, split peas and stock in a saucepan over medium–high heat and cook for 40 minutes until tender. Transfer into a food processor, add the preserved orange peel and ginger and purée until smooth. Check and adjust the seasoning as required. Set aside.

To serve, divide the veal between the serving plates and sprinkle with the almonds, parsley and lemon zest, place the purée in a separate bowl and serve.

Note You can also cook this dish in a pressure cooker. The meat will cook in about half the time.

### Veal shin and saffron

2 kg (4 lb 8 oz) cut veal shanks
pinch of saffron threads
1 teaspoon saffron powder
1 tablespoon ground cumin
60 ml (2 fl oz/¼ cup) olive oil
6 red onions, thinly sliced
4 garlic cloves
2 preserved lemon peel strips
250 ml (9 fl oz/1 cup) dry white wine
500 ml (17 fl oz/2 cups) chicken stock

### Carrot and preserved orange purée

1 kg (2 lb 4 oz) carrots, peeled
2 brown onions, quartered
250 g (9 oz) dried split peas
500 ml (17 fl oz/2 cups) chicken stock
1 preserved orange*, peel only
4 cm (1½ inch) piece fresh ginger

handful almonds, roughly chopped, to serve
1 tablespoon chopped flat-leaf (Italian) parsley leaves, to serve
zest of 1 lemon, to serve

# PRESERVED LEMON AND DESERT VEGETABLE MEDFOUNA

**Delicious fillings wrapped in bread, what's not to love? Medfouna is a traditional Moroccan dish made with lamb and beef, and the ones I ate in Morocco were winners on all levels. Here's my version using a vegetable filling instead of meat.**

Preheat the oven to 100°C (200°F/Gas ½). Line a baking tray with baking paper.

Remove the pith and pulp from the preserved lemons and discard. Place the skins flat on the prepared tray and bake for 3 hours or until dried out. Remove from the oven and leave to cool, then blitz in a food processor to make a powder. Set aside until ready to serve.

Mix the sugar and yeast in a jug (pitcher) with 250 ml (9 fl oz/1 cup) of lukewarm water and allow to sit for 10 minutes until the yeast bubbles.

Mix the flours and salt together in a bowl, by hand. Add the activated yeast and water with the milk. Knead until soft and smooth. Cover with a tea towel (dish towel) and leave to rest for 20 minutes.

Knead the dough for 10 minutes, adding extra flour if the mixture is sticky. Divide the dough into 4 portions. Cover and allow to rise until almost doubled.

Preheat the oven to 200°C (400°F/Gas 6).

To make the vegetable filling, heat the olive oil in a heavy-based frying pan over medium–high heat. Add the onions and cook for about 20 minutes, until caramelised. Remove from the heat.

Mix all the vegetable filling ingredients together, including the caramelised onion, in a bowl. Check the seasoning and adjust as necessary.

When the dough is ready, sprinkle your work surface with a mixture of the coarse semolina, poppy seeds and crushed coriander seeds.

Divide each dough portion in half to make 8 portions, then roll out each piece of dough on the seeds, into 2 thin circles about the size of a side plate with one piece slightly larger than the other. Divide the filling into four and put a filling portion on a larger dough piece, leaving some room around the edge. Place a smaller dough piece on top, fold over and seal the edges. Repeat with the remaining dough pieces and filling.

Heat some olive oil in a frying pan over high heat and cook, in batches, for 3 minutes on each side. Remove from the heat, place on a baking tray and bake for 10 minutes until golden. Sprinkle the medfouna with 1 tablespoon of the reserved preserved lemon powder and serve.

4 preserved lemons
1 teaspoon sugar
7 g (⅕ oz) dried yeast
300 g (10½ oz/2 cups) plain (all-purpose) flour, plus extra for dusting
150 g (5½ oz/1 cup) wholemeal (whole-wheat) flour
1 teaspoon salt
80 ml (2½ fl oz/⅓ cup) milk
2 tablespoons coarse semolina
2 tablespoons poppy seeds
2 tablespoons crushed coriander seeds
olive oil, for frying

## Vegetable filling

100 ml (3½ fl oz) olive oil
6 onions, thinly sliced
2 tomatoes, grated
1 tablespoon finely diced preserved lemon peel
460 g (1 lb/2 cups) fresh ricotta cheese
2 zucchini (courgettes), grated
1 tablespoon smoked paprika
handful coriander (cilantro), leaves picked and roughly chopped
handful flat-leaf (Italian) parsley, leaves picked and roughly chopped

# CLEMENTINE AND SAFFRON MARMALADE

**Clementine oranges are so undervalued. They should be eaten by the kilogram when in season, and this is one of the best recipes I know of to preserve them for the months when you can't find them and you crave them! The mix of saffron with the sweet tang of the clementine is pure gold.**

Remove the peel from the clementines and thinly slice the peel. Place the fruit segments, along with the peel in a large glass bowl, add 2 litres (70 fl oz/8 cups) of water and the lemon juice, cover and set aside to soak overnight.

Pour the clementines and soaking liquid into a large stockpot and bring to the boil over high heat. Add the sugar and stir to dissolve. Add the saffron. Return to the boil and continue to cook for about 40 minutes, until the marmalade jells when tested on a cold plate. To test for setting, place a small plate in the freezer. Place a drop of marmalade on the saucer and return to the freezer for 1 minute. Test by running your finger through the marmalade. If it wrinkles and forms a skin, it is ready. Pour the marmalade into hot sterilised jars and seal.

Note Clementine and saffron marmalade can be stored for 12 months, unopened, in the pantry.

Serve on toast as part of a breakfast feast.

1 kg (2 lb 4 oz) clementines
   (or mandarins)
2 tablespoons lemon juice
1.1 kg (2 lb 7 oz/5 cups) sugar
pinch of saffron threads

# ORANGE GROVE BEGHRIR WITH ORANGE BLOSSOM YOGHURT

Traditional beghrir are a kind of 'crumplet'—a mix between a crumpet and a pikelet. I loved it when I tasted it in Morocco. What I did when I came home was take the best bit of the Beghrir, which was the crunchy semolina base, and brought it to this recipe. It worked a treat and now this is a dish you will find in the Delia house every Sunday morning for breakfast. They are so easy to make and, let me tell you, once you have cooked them once, it won't be your last.

Mix the yoghurt with the orange blossom water in a small bowl. Line a fine mesh sieve with muslin (cheesecloth) and place over a bowl. Drain the yoghurt for a few hours until thickened.

Put the yeast and sugar in a bowl, then whisk in 300 ml (10½ fl oz) of lukewarm water. Set aside in a warm spot for 15 minutes or until frothy.

Put the flour, semolina, cream of tartar, salt and milk in the bowl of an electric stand mixer. Add the activated yeast and mix with the dough hook at low speed for about 8 minutes until a dough forms. Cover with a tea towel (dish towel) and leave the mixture to prove for 1 hour or until it starts to form bubbles. Add the bicarbonate of soda and mix for a further 2 minutes at a moderate speed to incorporate.

To cook the beghrir, oil four egg rings with a pastry brush and place in a frying pan over medium heat. Sprinkle some semolina in each ring. Pour the beghrir mixture into the egg rings, cook on one side for about 5 minutes, until holes form on the surface and the top has begun to set. Flip over and cook on the other side for 1–2 minutes more. Repeat with the remaining batter to make 8 beghrir.

Serve with clementine marmalade and the orange blossom yoghurt.

*Notes* The semolina gives added texture to the base of the beghrir when you are cooking them. You can use a skewer to aid the holes forming in the tops of the beghrir, before turning to cook on the other side.

500 g (1 lb 2 oz) Greek-style yoghurt
1–2 tablespoons orange blossom water*
7 g (⅕ oz) sachet dried yeast
½ teaspoon caster (superfine) sugar
240 g (8½ oz) plain (all-purpose) flour
130 g (4½ oz/⅔ cup) coarse semolina, plus extra for dusting (see note)
½ teaspoon cream of tartar
1 teaspoon salt
200 ml (7 fl oz) lukewarm milk
½ teaspoon bicarbonate of soda (baking soda)
1 tablespoon olive oil
clementine marmalade (see page 199), to serve

# MINT AND APPLE PASTILLA WITH DATE AND RAS EL HANOUT ICE CREAM

I don't know anyone who doesn't love an apple pie. This recipe has everything you need in an apple pie—gooey apple filling, caramelised apple flavours, crispy pastry and just enough spice to wake you up and make it interesting.

I really wanted to pay homage to the original pastille. It is such a wonderful dish that is loved by so many people. I think this dish has done that. It's not pretending to be authentic, but what it has is the soul and complexity of texture that the original has.

But the real winner of this dish is the ice cream! Do yourself a favour and make a big batch of it because once you taste it you won't want to stop eating it. It is one of the best ice creams I have ever made.

### DATE AND RAS EL HANOUT ICE CREAM

Put the sugar and 250 ml (9 fl oz/1 cup) of water in a saucepan over low heat and stir gently to dissolve. Remove from the heat, add the dates and purée until smooth using a hand-held stick blender. Set aside to cool.

Beat the egg yolks using an electric stand mixer with the whisk attachment on moderate–high speed until thick and pale. Add to the cooled date purée.

Whip the cream in a separate bowl to soft peaks with the whisk attachment. Fold the date purée and egg yolk mixture into the cream. Season with ras el hanout to taste, transfer into a container and freeze for 2–3 hours.

### MINT CRÈME

Heat the milk in a small saucepan over high heat, then remove from the heat add the mint leaves and leave for 10 minutes to infuse. Pour the mixture through a sieve, discard the mint leaves and return the infused milk to the pan. Add the remaining ingredients to the pan and whisk over medium–low heat for 15 minutes until thick. Place the mixture in a piping (icing) bag and set aside.

### APPLE PASTILLA

Heat 50 g (1¾ oz) of the butter in a frying pan over medium heat and sprinkle over the caster sugar. Stir until dissolved, then reduce the heat to low, add the apples and cook for about 20 minutes, turning occasionally, until soft and burnished in colour. Remove from the heat and set aside.

## Date and ras el hanout ice cream

175 g (6 oz) caster (superfine) sugar

12 medjool dates, pitted

8 egg yolks

1 litre (35 fl oz/4 cups) thickened (whipping) cream

2 tablespoons ras el hanout*

## Mint crème

670 ml (23 fl oz/2⅔ cups) milk

large handful mint, leaves picked

1 vanilla bean, split and seeds scraped

3 tablespoons cornflour (cornstarch)

65 g (2¼ oz/⅓ cup) semolina

150 g (5½ oz/⅔ cup) caster (superfine) sugar

2 eggs

few drops mint essence

## Apple pastilla

175 g (6 oz) butter

110 g (3¾ oz/½ cup) caster (superfine) sugar

3 golden delicious apples, peeled, cored and cut into wedges

100 g (3½ oz) whole almonds, toasted and roughly chopped

100 g (3½ oz) icing (confectioners') sugar, plus extra for dusting

1 tablespoon ground cinnamon

8 sheets filo pastry (see note)

mint leaves, to serve

Preheat the oven to 200°C (400°F/Gas 6). Line a baking tray with baking paper. Melt the remaining 125 g (4½ oz) of butter in the microwave.

Mix the almonds, icing sugar and cinnamon together in a bowl. Set aside.

Take a sheet of filo pastry and brush with butter. Sprinkle with some of the almond mixture and top with another sheet of filo. Using a 9 cm (3½ inch) round cutter, cut out eight circles. Repeat this step with the remaining pastry and almond mixture. You will have 32 circles.

Place four 9 cm ring moulds on a baking tray lined with baking paper.

Place one circle of filo in the bottom of each mould, brush with melted butter and sprinkle over some almond mixture. Overlap four circles in a petal pattern around the inside of each mould, to cover the sides, so it overhangs the edge evenly, and gently brush with butter. Place another circle of filo in each mould to hold the four circles of pastry in position. Place some apple filling in each mould.

Pipe in enough mint crème to cover. Place one round of filo on top of each, brush with butter and sprinkle with the almond mix. Fold over the pastry petals neatly. Brush the top with melted butter, sprinkle with almond mix and top with the last filo circle. Bake in the oven for 30 minutes or until the pastry is brown and crisp.

Remove the pastilla from the oven and remove the ring moulds. Rest for 5 minutes then invert onto a plate.

## TO SERVE

Dust the apple pastilla with icing sugar and place on four individual plates. Add a scoop of date and ras el hanout ice cream and serve.

Note It is important to prevent the filo pastry from drying out. Keep it covered with a clean cloth until you need it. Brush with plenty of melted butter to keep it pliable.

Mint and apple pastilla with date and ras el hanout ice cream

Preparation time: 20 minutes • Cooking time: 30 minutes • Serves: 8

# CHOCOLATE AND PISTACHIO M'HENCHA

**Bringing together the techniques and flavours of the old and new schools—this dish was a meld of the refined Moroccan–French food I saw at the Selman hotel in Marrakesh and the old-school beauty of a traditional m'hencha (a type of pastry cake). The flavour combination that resulted was something that I am definitely going to put on the menu at Maha. I love the way the ginger comes into play with this dish.**

200 g (7 oz) dark chocolate
350 g (12 oz) pistachio nuts
130 g (4½ oz) palm sugar
pinch of saffron powder
1 tablespoon ground ginger
115 g (4 oz) butter, melted
8 sheets filo pastry

Put the chocolate, pistachios, palm sugar, saffron, ginger and 2 tablespoons of the melted butter in a food processor and blend until finely ground (see note).

Preheat the oven to 180°C (350°F/Gas 4). Line a baking tray with baking paper.

Open out the sheets of filo, keeping them in a pile so they don't dry out. Take 1 sheet and brush with a little melted butter.

Take lumps of the chocolate nut paste and roll into fingers. Place them end to end on the top sheet of filo, then roll the filo up into a roll the thickness of your thumb, tucking in the ends. Repeat with the other filo sheets, until the filling is used up.

Press the filo rolls together from both ends, like an accordion, to relax the pastry before coiling it to make 8 small coils on the prepared baking tray.

Brush some extra butter over the pastry, then bake for 30 minutes or until golden and crisp.

*Notes* The filling can be made 1 day ahead of time and refrigerated until required.

You can substitute different flavours for the filling, such as almonds, hazelnuts and walnuts.

# DATE, ORANGE AND OLIVE OIL CAKE WITH SALTED WHITE CHOCOLATE ICE CREAM

The palm groves of Morocco are breathtaking. Kilometres of trees producing some of the most high quality dates I have ever seen. On my travels, some Bedouin men showed me that if you warm dates in olive oil before placing them in a tagine it helps bring out the flavour of the caramel in the date. This got me thinking, and led to this recipe.

## SALTED WHITE CHOCOLATE ICE CREAM

Put the sugar and 250 ml (9 fl oz/1 cup) of water in a saucepan over low heat to dissolve. Add the white chocolate and mix until smooth. Remove from the heat and set aside to cool.

Beat the egg yolks using an electric stand mixer with a paddle attachment at moderate–high speed until thick and pale, then add to the cooled chocolate.

Whip the cream to stiff peaks in the mixer with the whisk attachment.

Fold the chocolate into the cream using a spatula. Season with salt to taste.

Pour the mixture into a container and freeze for 2–3 hours.

## DATE, ORANGE AND OLIVE OIL CAKE

Mix the breadcrumbs, almond meal, caster sugar, ras el hanout and baking powder together in a bowl.

Whisk the eggs together in a bowl with the olive oil. Add the zests and stir to combine. Fold the egg mixture into the breadcrumb mixture until just combined.

Line a 21 x 11 cm (8¼ x 4¼ inch) loaf (bar) tin with baking paper and pour in the mixture. Place the cake in a cold oven and turn on to 170°C (325°F/Gas 3). Bake for 45 minutes or until the cake is cooked when tested with a skewer and is golden.

Put the remaining ingredients in a saucepan over high heat. Bring to the boil then reduce the heat and simmer for a few minutes. Remove from the heat.

Remove the cake from the oven and pierce all over with a wooden skewer. Drizzle over the spiced syrup and leave for a few minutes to soak up the syrup.

## TO SERVE

Remove the salted white chocolate ice cream from the freezer and leave to soften slightly. Cut the cake into slices and serve warm or cold with the ice cream.

*Note* You can use different shaped tins instead of the loaf tin. If so, you may need to adjust the cooking time.

### Salted white chocolate ice cream

175 g (6 oz) caster (superfine) sugar
500 g (1 lb 2 oz) white chocolate buttons
8 egg yolks
1 litre (35 fl oz/4 cups) thickened (whipping) cream
pinch of sea salt

### Date, orange and olive oil cake

50 g (1¾ oz) panko breadcrumbs
125 g (4½ oz/1¼ cup) almond meal
220 g (7¾ oz/1 cup) caster (superfine) sugar
1 teaspoon ras el hanout*
1 teaspoon baking powder
4 eggs
250 ml (9 fl oz/1 cup) olive oil
zest of 1 lemon
zest of 1 orange
2 tablespoons lemon juice
80 ml (2½ fl oz/⅓ cup) orange juice
55 g (2 oz/¼ cup) sugar
6 medjool dates, pitted
1 cinnamon stick
8–10 cardamom pods
2 star anise

# ARGAN OIL CHOCOLATE MUD BROWNIE WITH ORANGE CINNAMON ICE CREAM

After every meal in Morocco I was presented with a plate of freshly cut oranges dusted with cinnamon. While a great flavour combination in its own right, when turned into an ice cream and paired with this brownie it's become a killer recipe that will have chocolate lovers begging for more.

### ARGAN OIL CHOCOLATE MUD BROWNIE

Preheat the oven to 160°C (315°F/Gas 2–3). Line a baking tray with baking paper.

Put the white and milk chocolate buttons on the prepared tray and bake for 10–15 minutes until combined and caramelised. Remove from the oven and set aside to cool, then break up into smaller pieces.

Mix the eggs and sugar in an electric stand mixer with the whisk attachment for 5 minutes on moderate–high speed or until soft peaks form. Set aside.

Melt the dark chocolate with the butter then stir in the argan oil. Add the dark chocolate mixture to the eggs and sugar and mix well until combined. Add the sour cream, cocoa powder, baking powder and salt and fold through with the broken up pieces of caramelised chocolate.

Grease a 21 x 11 cm (8¼ x 4¼ inch) loaf (bar) tin. Pour in the mixture and bake for 45 minutes or until a skewer comes out clean and the top is slightly cracked.

### ORANGE AND CINNAMON ICE CREAM

Heat the orange juice, zest and sugar in a saucepan over low heat, stirring to dissolve the sugar. Remove from the heat and set aside to cool.

Beat the egg yolks in a bowl with a whisk and add to the cooled orange mixture. Add the vanilla seeds, cinnamon and orange extract.

Whip the cream to soft peaks using an electric stand mixer with a whisk attachment. Fold the orange mixture into the cream.

Pour the combined mixture into a container and freeze for 2–3 hours. Allow to soften slightly before serving.

### TO SERVE

Cut the argan oil chocolate mud brownie into slices and serve with a scoop of orange and cinnamon ice cream.

*Note* You can also make this brownie in a traditional brownie tin. It will take less time to cook. Try adding nuts for a different flavour and texture.

## Argan oil chocolate mud brownie

75 g (2½ oz) white chocolate buttons
75 g (2½ oz) milk chocolate buttons
3 eggs
230 g (8 oz) light brown sugar
200 g (7 oz) dark chocolate
60 g (2¼ oz) butter
60 ml (2 fl oz/¼ cup) argan oil*
75 g (2½ oz) sour cream
30 g (1 oz/¼ cup) dark cocoa powder
1 teaspoon baking powder
pinch of salt

## Orange and cinnamon ice cream

250 ml (9 fl oz/1 cup) orange juice
grated zest of 2 oranges
130 g (4½ oz) sugar
8 egg yolks
1 vanilla bean, split and seeds scraped
2 teaspoons ground cinnamon
2 teaspoons orange extract
1 litre (35 fl oz/4 cups) thickened (whipping) cream

Vejer de la Frontera

# ANDALUCÍA
## SPAIN

I have often wondered during my travels around the Middle East how it was possible for the once awe-inspiring art, medicine, education and architecture in this region to be so far ahead of the West and then suddenly just stop and, if anything, go backwards.

On my Moorish spice journey, travelling from Morocco to Andalucía, a part of modern Spain, this question was once again rolling around in my mind. Don't get me wrong, I loved Morocco. The hustle and bustle, excitement and energy in the street, beautiful people and landscape, but to see where Morocco is today and what became of Andalucía since the Moors were kicked out almost 600 years ago, is nothing less than astonishing.

Every country I have travelled to I have been repeatedly stopped in my tracks by reminders of a past glory and opulence. Breathtaking mosques and palaces in Iran and Turkey, the world's first universities in North Africa. I heard people talk about the wisdom and science that emerged from the Middle Eastern Islamic world—poets, artists, and a refined and civilised way of life surrounded by beauty, tranquillity and balance—forward-thinking people who were the leaders and pioneers of their day.

It seems the best of what was brought by the Moors, who ruled this part of Spain for almost 800 years, had been picked up and taken to a new level when it crossed the Straits of Gibraltar. This pocket at the bottom of Spain embraced all the beauty and splendour of Moorish culture and ran with it—expanding on the Moorish ideals and achieving harmony and balance. I am in love with Andalucía in every way. There is a real sense of community, family and tradition paired with a relaxed way of life that really appeals to me.

As soon as I touched down in Jerez I felt relaxed. The air was bright, the light dazzling and there was a hum in the streets that didn't come from traffic or the commotion of people rushing about as it does back at home in Melbourne—it was a gentle, soothing hum of happiness that seemed to be bouncing all around the town.

My first meal—the first tapas bar I stepped into that night—was amazing. Real food cooked by real people and eaten by diners going about their everyday business. It wasn't a special night out, it was just dinner time. There was nobody instagramming their dishes, no one critiquing their meal on TripAdvisor or looking over their shoulder to see who was looking at them or who was at the next table. It was just people getting together and enjoying life—people just happy to be there.

BAY OF BISCAY

SPAIN

PORTUGAL

✖ Cordoba

Seville ♣ ANDALUCÍA

Jerez ✖ Malaga ✖ Granada
✖
✖ Vejer de la
Frontera

Straits of Gibraltar

N

MOROCCO

Later, I walked down a street and found myself irresistibly drawn into a peña (folk club) by the wail of singing and guitars, and the lustful rhythm of flamenco, belting out stories of new and lost love. WOW, I thought, is this really what life can be?

Next stop Vejer de la Frontera. Let me just say through my whole spice journey life I have been looking for a place I could call home, and this town could well be it. Situated about an hour's drive from the closest airport, 30 minutes to the beach, and about a two-hour drive to Seville this 1400-year-old fortified town looks, for all its worth, like a whole tonne of sugar cubes has been scattered over the top of a hill. From it, you can see the rolling green fields of the Cadiz countryside and on the horizon the glittering Straits of Gibraltar and the coastline of Morocco. And along its winding roads and impossibly narrow lanes, tiny hidden tapas bars, markets and fabulous food shops run by the producers themselves.

I continued on my Andalucían odyssey—up and down the coast and all through the middle, visiting some beautiful cities and witnessing a food scene that is alive and pumping. Chefs at every level living for what they do and passionately sharing their craft with anyone who wants to experience it. There's everything from local working-class tapas bars that produce the best pork-stuffed rolls you have ever tasted, to a place that the king of modern Spanish cuisine, Ferran Adrià, and the actual king of Spain go to munch on crunchy prawn tortillitas. Even at the top of the tree where new world chefs cook with Spanish flair and bravado, they seem to share a brotherhood and respect for each other's skill and the dishes they create.

Comrades rather than competitors, this mindset is evident among local farmers who have such a strong connection with their land and crops, and the fishermen of Barbate fishing the same sea my Phoenician ancestors did, using the same ancient fishing techniques. It's also evident among the jamón producers in the Sierra de Aracena whose dehesa (oak forest) provides the perfect living environment for Iberian pigs that become heavenly jamón iberico de bellota.

This is what is exciting about Andalucía. What they have is perfect just as it is, but instead of being complacent and leaving things the way they are, they look for new and inspiring ways to make the most of things. Not for money or glory, but because they can, because they should and because their souls yearn for more for tomorrow than they have today. ✖

*Let me just say through my whole spice journey life I have been looking for a place I could call my home, and this town could well be it.*

# TARTARE OF TUNA, HARISSA AIOLI WITH SPICED WAFER

Tuna is a big deal all over the world and it is no different in Spain. Especially in the Straits of Gibraltar where tuna fishing has been an art since the time of the Phoenicians. These guys take their tuna fishing and cooking very seriously and no part of the fish is wasted. In my opinion, tuna is best eaten raw, simply dressed, where the natural texture and flavour of the fish do all the talking.

This dish pays homage to the flavours of Andalucía and the great tuna fishermen along the southern shore. The mojama brings a salty, strong fishy flavour into play, which works really well with the fresh tuna tartare.

Mix all the harissa aioli ingredients together in a bowl.

Put the tuna in a bowl and add a few spoonfuls of the harissa aioli to loosely bind. Add the remaining ingredients and mix together. Place in the fridge to chill.

Preheat the oven to 180°C (350°F/Gas 4).

Brush the pastry with the olive oil and place on a baking tray. Finely grate the almonds with a microplane over the top and scatter over the remaining ingredients, except the mojama. Bake for 15 minutes or until golden.

Place a spoonful of the tuna on each plate. Dollop over some harissa aioli. Surround with shards of brik pastry and grate over the mojama.

**Notes** This is a great dish for when you're entertaining, as it's quick and easy to make the tuna.

Mojama is a salt-cured tuna. You only need a small amount as it packs a big punch. It is available at specialty food stores. It can also be purchased online.

### Harissa aioli
235 g (8½ oz/1 cup) aioli
    (or mayonnaise)
1 tablespoon harissa*
1 teaspoon smoked paprika

### Tartare of tuna
400 g (14 oz) sashimi-grade tuna,
    diced
90 g (3¼ oz/½ cup) Spanish green
    olives, pitted and diced
2 French shallots, diced
2 tablespoons chopped chives
pinch of sea salt
80 ml (2½ fl oz/⅓ cup) olive oil

### Spiced wafer
4 sheets brik pastry*
olive oil, for brushing
25 g (1 oz/¼ cup) blanched almonds
1 tablespoon thyme leaves
1 tablespoon coriander seeds,
    crushed
zest of 2 lemons
20 g (¾ oz) mojama (see note)

Preparation time: 10 minutes plus 2 hours chilling • Cooking time: nil • Serves: 4

# MOORISH CHILLED ALMOND AND ORANGE BLOSSOM SOUP WITH APPLE AND WATERCRESS DRESSING

This is a great soup, awesome on a hot summer's day. I couldn't believe how easy it was and for a dish with such ancient origins, how beautiful and complex the flavour profile could be.

Put the almonds, garlic, bread and apple in a food processor and whiz until a paste is formed. With the motor running, slowly add 200 ml (7 fl oz) of water, then add the olive oil and 1½ tablespoons of the sherry vinegar. Next, add the orange blossom water, adjusting to taste if necessary. Season with salt, then pour into a jug (pitcher) and refrigerate for 2 hours to chill.

Finely chop the prawns and mix in a bowl with the chilli, coriander, lemon zest, salt to taste and the remaining vinegar. Drizzle with olive oil. Cover and refrigerate for 30 minutes to cure.

Make the dressing by mixing together the apple, almonds, chives and watercress with enough olive oil to coat and salt to season.

Place the chilled soup in individual bowls, add the prawns and finish with the apple and watercress dressing and a drizzle of olive oil.

Note You can grill or sauté the prawns if you prefer them cooked.

100 g (3½ oz) blanched almonds
1 garlic clove
2 thick slices day-old bread, soaked in water until soft
½ green apple, peeled, quartered and chopped
100 ml (3½ fl oz) extra virgin olive oil, plus 1 tablespoon extra
90 ml (3 fl oz) sherry vinegar
1 teaspoon orange blossom water*
pinch of sea salt
8 large raw prawn (shrimp), peeled and deveined, tails removed (see note)
1 small red chilli, seeds removed, diced
1 tablespoon finely chopped coriander (cilantro) leaves
zest of 1 lemon

### Apple and watercress dressing
1 green apple, peeled, cored and finely diced
handful flaked almonds
1 tablespoon chopped chives
handful watercress, leaves picked
drizzle of extra virgin olive oil
pinch of sea salt

# SALMOREJO PURÉE WITH JAMON, QUAIL EGG, GREEN APPLE AND SHERRY DRESSING

I was a bit sceptical about this dish before I ate it. I thought what is all the fuss about? It's just a thick gazpacho, how good could it be? Well, let me tell you it is the bomb!

Instead of making the salmorejo the star of the show I have turned it into a refresher of sorts and turned up the flavours that accompany this great dish.

I hope I have done it some justice.

### PICKLED QUAIL EGGS

Combine all the ingredients except the eggs in a small saucepan over medium heat. Bring to the boil, then simmer for 3 minutes. Remove from the heat and leave to cool.

Place the eggs in a sterilised jar and pour over the vinegar mixture. Refrigerate for 24 hours before using.

### SALMOREJO PURÉE

Place all the ingredients in a food processor and blend until thick and smooth. Check and adjust the seasoning to taste.

### ALMOND PURÉE

Put the almonds and milk in a saucepan over medium heat and cook for 20 minutes or until the almonds are soft. Remove from the heat and blend in a food processor until silky smooth. Blend in the olive oil and sherry vinegar to taste.

### SPICY PORK

Heat the olive oil and jamon fat in a frying pan over medium heat. Add the pork mince, bay leaf, paprika, onion and garlic, and cook until the pork is crispy. Remove and set aside.

### Pickled quail eggs

120 ml (3¾ fl oz) white wine vinegar
60 ml (2 fl oz/¼ cup) dry white wine
1 teaspoon fennel seeds
1 teaspoon coriander seeds
1 teaspoon black peppercorns
½ teaspoon smoked paprika
½ teaspoon sea salt
2 French shallots, sliced
1 bay leaf
6 boiled quail eggs, peeled (see note)

### Salmorejo purée

4 tomatoes, chopped
1 green capsicum (pepper), chopped
2 garlic cloves
2 slices bread, soaked in a little water
60 ml (2 fl oz/¼ cup) olive oil
dash of Tabasco
pinch of saffron threads
2 tablespoons sherry vinegar

### Almond purée

160 g (5½ oz/1 cup) blanched almonds
800 ml (28 fl oz) milk
125 ml (4 fl oz/½ cup) olive oil
2 tablespoons sherry vinegar

### Spicy pork

2 tablespoons olive oil
40 g (1½ oz) jamon fat
400 g (14 oz) minced (ground) pork
1 bay leaf
2 teaspoons smoked paprika
1 brown onion, diced
1 garlic clove, diced

### Sherry dressing

125 ml (4 fl oz/ ½ cup) Spanish sherry
2 French shallots, finely diced
1 teaspoon coriander seeds
2 tablespoons chopped toasted
   almonds
2 tablespoons chopped chives
1 tablespoon sherry vinegar
splash of olive oil

### To serve

8 thin jamon slices, torn
2 green apples, scooped into balls
handful baby radishes, thinly sliced
1 turnip, peeled and very thinly sliced
6 chives, cut into 3 cm (1¼ inch)
   lengths
handful frisee leaves

### SHERRY DRESSING

Put the sherry in a small saucepan over high heat. Bring to the boil and cook until the sherry has reduced by half. Add the shallots and coriander seeds, almonds, chives and sherry vinegar. Set aside to cool. When cool, add enough olive oil to make a dressing. Check and adjust the seasoning.

### TO SERVE

Place some almond purée around the base of each plate. Scatter over the crispy pork. Cut the quail eggs in half and place two halves on each plate. Scatter the jamon, apple, radish, turnip, chives and frisee around the rim of the plate and dress with some of the sherry dressing.

   Serve with small bowls of salmorejo.

**Notes** To ensure the yolks are centred in the eggs, stir them while in the boiling water. For a hard-boiled white with a soft runny yolk, put the eggs into a small saucepan of boiling water and cook for 2½ minutes. Remove and cool in iced water. Removing the shell is easier if the egg is cold.

Salmorejo purée with jamon, quail egg, green apple and sherry dressing

# POACHED LOBSTER PRINGA, WITH GAZPACHO-FLAVOURED MAYONNAISE AND PRAWN CRACKLING

There is no way in the world I could even begin to try to cook a pork pringa like the one I had in Seville. It was the best sandwich I have ever eaten, hands down.

I think what really caught me by surprise was the unsteadiness of this pringa. It just looked like a dry overcooked little bread roll with not much going on. Boy, was I wrong! Jammed into the middle of a crunchy moist little roll was fatty, salty meaty goodness that almost knocked me off my seat.

Anyway, this is my take. Like I said, I didn't want to try to imitate it, so I just drew on some of the textures and tried to bring out the flavours I chose to use. I hope you like it!

1 lobster tail (about 400–500 g/ 14 oz–1 lb 2 oz)
500 g (1 lb 2 oz) raw prawns (shrimp), peeled and roughly chopped
2 tablespoons plain (all-purpose) flour
canola oil, for deep-frying
2 tablespoons smoked paprika, for dusting
8 small bread rolls, halved
olive oil, for frying
handful watercress, leaves picked

## Gazpacho-flavoured mayonnaise
235 g (8½ oz/1 cup) mayonnaise
2 tablespoons tomato sauce (ketchup)
1 teaspoon Tabasco sauce
½ Lebanese (short) cucumber, peeled and finely diced
½ red onion, finely diced
6 flat-leaf (Italian) parsley stems, leaves picked and chopped
6 mint stems, leaves picked and chopped

To cook the lobster tail, place it in a small saucepan and cover with lightly salted water. Bring to the boil, reduce the heat to a simmer and cook for 8–12 minutes until the shell turns bright red and the meat is tender. For larger or smaller tails, adjust the cooking time as needed. Remove from the heat and drain.

Meanwhile, to make the gazpacho-flavoured mayonnaise, mix all the ingredients together in a bowl. Season with salt and freshly ground black pepper and set aside.

Remove the prawn meat from the shell, place the prawn meat in a bowl and coat lightly in the flour.

Pour some canola oil into a deep frying pan, about 4 cm (1½ inches) deep, then heat over medium–high heat until it shimmers. If you have a kitchen thermometer, the oil will be ready when the temperature reaches 180°C (350°F). Alternatively, use a deep-fryer.

Carefully add the prawn meat to the pan and deep-fry for a few minutes, until crisp and crunchy. Remove and drain on paper towel. Toss with some paprika to season.

Heat a frying pan over high heat. Drizzle the bread rolls with olive oil, season with salt and pepper and fry until crisp and crunchy on the outside.

Gently tear the lobster into bite-sized pieces. Place in a bowl and toss with some of the gazpacho-flavoured mayonnaise and watercress.

Fill the fried bread rolls with the lobster and mayo mixture, top with the prawns and serve immediately.

Note For a change, serve with small bowls of traditional gazpacho.

# OLIVE OIL POACHED POTATOES, PICKLED OCTOPUS AND GREEN OLIVES

This is a typical Spanish tapas that you will find all throughout Andalucía, although every tapas bar will have their own subtle little twist on it that makes it theirs.

This is my little twist—I think the introduction of octopus and some bitter orange zest gives it a slight edge over some of the ones I ate in Spain.

Place all the pickled octopus ingredients in a large non-metallic bowl with 500 ml (17 fl oz/2 cups) of water. Cover with plastic wrap and place in the fridge for 12 hours. Remove and drain. Discard the liquid.

Place the potatoes in a saucepan and cover with cold water. Add a pinch of salt, bring to the boil over medium–high heat and cook for 15 minutes or until tender when tested with a sharp knife. Remove from the heat, drain and break in half. Toss the potatoes in the olive oil and allow them to absorb the oil. Drizzle with the vinegar, season with salt and pepper and set aside.

Heat a grill pan over high heat. When hot, grill the octopus for a couple of minutes until charred and just cooked through. Season with salt and pepper. Remove and slice into bite-sized pieces.

Toss the octopus with the potatoes, add the olives, shallot, spring onions, garlic and parsley. Top with the seville orange zest and smoked paprika, and serve.

**Note** Kiwi fruit contains a natural enzyme that helps to tenderise the octopus.

### Pickled octopus

1 kg (2 lb 4 oz) baby octopus, cleaned, beaks removed
2½ tablespoons white vinegar
1 kiwi fruit, peeled and puréed (see note)
2 teaspoons salt
1 garlic clove, sliced
1 bay leaf
5 thyme sprigs
1 teaspoon smoked paprika

800 g (1 lb 12 oz) mixed potatoes (such as kipfler, desiree, purple)
250 ml (9 fl oz/1 cup) Spanish olive oil
2 tablespoons sherry vinegar
175 g (6 oz/1 cup) Spanish green olives, pitted and roughly chopped
1 French shallot, diced
4 spring onions (scallions), thinly sliced
1 large garlic clove
2 tablespoons chopped flat-leaf (Italian) parsley
zest of 1 seville orange
2 teaspoons smoked paprika

# BRAISED PIG'S EARS, MORCILLA, QUAIL EGGS AND JAMON

Tapas bars in Spain all have their own soul and personality. They have dishes they do well and then they have dishes that they do bloody well. The food in general in Andalucía is humblingly good. This dish is my homage to the flavours and products of good Spanish tapas.

### BRAISED PIG'S EARS

Bring a saucepan of water to the boil. Place the pig's ears in the water and parboil for a few minutes to remove any scum and impurities.

Remove the ears from the water and place in a clean saucepan. Add enough water to cover both ears. Add the onion, carrot, and herbs. Bring to the boil over medium–high heat, then reduce the heat and simmer for 2½ hours or until the ears are very soft. Remove from the pan and slice into strips.

### CARAMELISED ONION DRESSING

Cook the onions and olive oil in a wide heavy-based frying pan over low heat for about 30 minutes until golden and caramelised. Remove from the heat and allow to cool. Once cool, strain over a bowl, then finely chop the onions. Reserve the oil.

Put the chopped onions back into the oil and add the sherry vinegar and mustard to taste.

### ALMOND PURÉE

Put the almonds and milk in a saucepan over medium heat and cook for 20 minutes or until the almonds are soft. Remove from the heat and blend in a food processor until silky smooth. Blend in the olive oil and sherry vinegar to taste.

#### Braised pig's ears

2 pigs ears (about 80–100 g/
    2¾–3½ oz each)
1 onion, cut into large pieces
1 carrot, peeled and quartered
a few sprigs each of thyme, bay leaf
    and oregano

#### Caramelised onion dressing

2 brown onions, thinly sliced
250 ml (9 fl oz/1 cup) olive oil
60 ml (2 fl oz/¼ cup) sherry vinegar
1 teaspoon wholegrain mustard

#### Almond purée

80 g (2¾ oz/½ cup) blanched almonds
400 ml (14 fl oz) milk
60 ml (2 fl oz/¼ cup) olive oil
2 tablespoons sherry vinegar

#### To assemble

canola oil, for deep-frying
plain (all-purpose) flour, for dusting
2 tablespoons olive oil
1 morcilla sausage, sliced
1 slice day-old bread, torn into pieces
1 tablespoon smoked paprika
1 tablespoon sherry vinegar
handful flat-leaf (Italian) parsley,
    leaves picked and torn
2 tablespoons butter
4 quail eggs
8 thin slices jamon
100 g (3½ oz) mixed salad greens
    and watercress, to serve
extra virgin olive oil, to serve

## TO ASSEMBLE

Pour some canola oil into a deep frying pan, about 4 cm (1½ inches) deep, then heat over medium–high heat until it shimmers. If you have a kitchen thermometer, the oil will be ready when the temperature reaches 180°C (350°F). Alternatively, use a deep-fryer.

Dust the braised pig's ears in flour and deep fry for a few minutes until crispy and crunchy. Remove and drain on paper towel, sprinkle with salt and pepper to season.

Heat the olive oil in a medium frying pan over medium heat and fry the morcilla sausage until golden brown. Add the bread and cook in the sausage pan juices until golden and crunchy. Add 2 tablespoons of the onion dressing to the pan. Sprinkle over the paprika. Finish with the sherry vinegar and torn parsley.

In a separate frying pan, melt the butter over low heat and then gently fry the quail eggs until just cooked. Season with salt and pepper and set aside.

To serve, brush some almond purée across each plate. Layer some slices of jamon, top with pig's ears, the morcilla sausage and the croutons. Add the salad greens, drizzle over some extra virgin olive oil, and top with a fried quail egg.

Notes The caramelised onion dressing can be kept in the fridge for up to 1 week. The olive oil will become solid from refrigerating, so allow it to come to room temperature before using.

When braising the pig's ears, double the quantity and freeze the extra for next time.

You can use a pressure cooker to halve the cooking time for the pig's ears.

Braised pig's ears,
morcilla, quail eggs
and jamon

# KANGAROO DE TORO WITH ROAST JERUSALEM ARTICHOKES

**It's funny how this dish came about, I had just eaten the best rabo de toro in all of Andalucía and I was licking the plate it was so good. Then I got talking to the restaurant owner and he said they use the tails from bullfight bulls to make the dish. Now, irrespective of your political stance on bullfighting, this is an amazing dish and we started joking about how if we were to do it in Australia, maybe we could use a 'fighting kangaroo'? And then bang, this dish was born.**

Combine the paprika, saffron powder and nutmeg. Rub the mixture over the kangaroo to coat well.

Put the kangaroo in a heavy-based saucepan or flameproof casserole dish and place over high heat. Cook for a few minutes, turning occasionally to brown all over and seal the sides. Remove from the pan and set aside.

Heat the olive oil in the pan, then add the onions, pancetta, garlic, bay leaves, peppercorns, cinnamon sticks and cloves. Cook for 10 minutes, stirring occasionally until the onion is very soft. Deglaze with the sherry and reduce the liquid by half. Return the kangaroo to the pan, along with the tomato, and cover with about 500 ml (17 fl oz/2 cups) of water. Cover with a lid and cook for 1½ hours or until the meat is falling apart.

Meanwhile, put the artichokes, lemon juice, thyme, peppercorns, garlic, bay leaf and 1 litre (35 fl oz/4 cups) of water in a saucepan and bring to the boil over medium–high heat. Reduce the heat to low and simmer for 20 minutes or until the artichokes are soft when pierced with a sharp knife. Drain, then transfer to a tray lined with paper towel. Put in the fridge for 30 minutes to dry completely.

Preheat the oven to 200°C (400°F/Gas 6). Drizzle the oil into a roasting tin and place in the oven to heat.

Place the artichokes in the hot roasting tin and carefully toss through the oil. Cook for 30 minutes until golden and crunchy, turning as required.

Remove the artichokes from the oven and place in a large frying pan with a little extra oil over high heat. Add the Aleppo pepper, smoked paprika, parsley and lemon zest, and toss to combine the flavours for a few minutes. Season with salt and the sherry vinegar.

To serve, plate up the kangaroo and serve with the roasted artichokes.

**Note** Other red meats would be a good substitute in this dish.

## Kangaroo de Toro

2 teaspoon smoked paprika

1 g (⅒₅ oz) saffron powder

1 nutmeg, finely grated

1 kg (2 lb 4 oz) kangaroo tail pieces (see note)

2 tablespoons olive oil

500 g (1 lb 2 oz) onions, chopped

400 g (14 oz) flat pancetta, skin removed, chopped

1 garlic bulb, halved crossways

3 bay leaves

1 teaspoon black peppercorns, crushed

3 cinnamon sticks

10 cloves

450 ml (16 fl oz) Oloroso sherry

600 g (1 lb 5 oz) tomatoes, grated

## Roast Jerusalem artichokes

1 kg (2 lb 4 oz) Jerusalem artichokes, scrubbed and halved

2 tablespoons lemon juice

a few thyme sprigs

1 tablespoon black peppercorns

2 garlic cloves

1 bay leaf

80 ml (2½ fl oz/⅓ cup) olive oil, plus extra for frying

1 teaspoon red Aleppo pepper* (pul biber)

1 teaspoon smoked paprika

2 handfuls flat-leaf (Italian) parsley, leaves picked

zest of 1 lemon

2 tablespoons sherry vinegar

# BRAISED RABBIT WITH ARTICHOKE AND PEA SALAD

My new food hero Charo Carmona of Arte de Cozina in Antequera has touched my heart in a way no other cook has. She is a real foodie who has dedicated her life to the preservation of the food culture of her region. She not only cooks the food of her homeland, but works with producers to ensure the products she needs are still grown in their natural habitats so future generations can enjoy the cuisine of this great food region.

Her passion for the food she cooked for me made every mouthful taste even better and, to be honest, I never wanted to leave her kitchen. This is one of the dishes she shared with me.

I hope I can make it back to Antequera one day and spend a whole day eating and drinking in Charo's restaurant.

Remove the belly flaps from the rabbit and reserve. Cut the rabbit into 8 pieces.

Put the olive oil and sliced garlic in a heavy-based saucepan over low heat and gently cook. When the garlic starts to turn golden, remove from the oil and set aside.

Increase the heat to medium, add the rabbit liver, kidneys and chicken liver to the pan and cook for 2–3 minutes until browned. Remove and set aside.

Reduce the heat to low, add the rabbit pieces and cook for 10 minutes, turning occasionally until evenly browned. Season with salt and freshly ground white pepper. Add the paprika and stir well. Add the onions, cinnamon sticks, bay leaf and saffron powder. Increase the heat to high and deglaze the pan with the sherry vinegar. Cook for a few minutes to reduce. Cover with about 1 litre (35 fl oz/4 cups) of boiling water and simmer for 45 minutes or until the meat falls off the bone.

Meanwhile, cook the artichoke hearts in a saucepan of lightly salted boiling water over medium–high heat for 20 minutes or until tender. (You can also boil or steam the leaves for another use.) Remove from the pan and set aside.

Use a mallet to flatten the rabbit flaps, slice thinly and season with salt and freshly ground black pepper. Rest for 10 minutes.

Wash the salt off the rabbit flaps, pat dry with paper towel and dust lightly with flour.

Pour some canola oil into a deep frying pan, about 4 cm (1½ inches) deep, then heat over medium–high heat until it shimmers. If you have a kitchen

## Braised rabbit

1 large farmed rabbit (about 2 kg/ 4 lb 8 oz), liver and kidneys reserved

500 ml (17 fl oz/2 cups) olive oil

1 garlic bulb, peeled and thinly sliced

200 g (7 oz) chicken livers

2 tablespoons smoked paprika

2 brown onions, sliced

2 cinnamon sticks

1 bay leaf

1 teaspoon saffron powder

250 ml (9 fl oz/1 cup) sherry vinegar

1 loaf day-old bread, cut into large chunks

## Artichoke and pea salad

4 small globe artichoke hearts

reserved rabbit belly flaps (see above)

2 tablespoons plain (all-purpose) flour

canola oil, for deep-frying

100 g (3½ oz) toasted almonds, roughly chopped

100 ml (3½ fl oz) olive oil

1 tablespoon lemon juice

1 small frisee, leaves picked

250 g (9 oz) fresh peas

1 kg (2 lb 4 oz) broad (fava) beans, double podded

6 slices jamon

thermometer, the oil will be ready when the temperature reaches 180°C (350°F). Alternatively, use a deep-fryer.

Carefully put the rabbit flaps in the oil and deep-fry for a few minutes until crunchy. Remove and drain on paper towel.

Using the same deep frying pan, carefully add the bread to the pan and deep fry for a few minutes until golden. Transfer onto paper towel to drain.

Meanwhile, remove the rabbit pieces from the saucepan, leave to cool slightly, then pick the meat from the bones. Set aside the meat and discard the bones. Reserve the cooking liquid.

Add the fried bread to the reserved rabbit cooking liquid with the cooked garlic, kidneys and livers. Transfer into a food processor and purée until thick and creamy. Adjust the seasoning. Return to the pan, fold through the picked meat and cover with a lid.

Combine the almonds, olive oil and lemon juice in a small bowl to make a dressing. Place the frisee in a salad bowl with the artichoke, peas, broad beans and belly. Scatter over the jamon and toss through the dressing.

Divide the braised rabbit between eight serving plates and serve with the artichoke and pea salad.

Note This recipe only uses the artichoke heart, but you can keep the leaves for another use. Trim off the leaves and scoop out the hairy 'choke' and discard. You can stop the artichoke from discolouring by placing it in a bowl of water with half a lemon.

Braised rabbit
with artichoke
and pea salad

Preparation time: 20 minutes • Cooking time: 50 minutes • Serves: 4

# SQUID INK RICE WITH CHORIZO-FILLED BABY CALAMARI AND SEAWEED

I remember cooking squid ink risotto as a commis chef and falling in love with it back then, so to see it again was like falling in love all over again. The introduction of the nori was a great little touch, which I loved, and chorizo is a winner with any type of seafood in my book.

Heat 2 tablespoons of the olive oil in a frying pan over medium–high heat. Add the chorizo and cook for a few minutes, turning often until well coloured and crisp. Add the cuttlefish, parsley and chilli and toss to combine. Continue to cook until the cuttlefish is opaque and just cooked. Remove the chorizo mixture from the pan, transfer into a bowl and leave to cool.

Place 110 g (3¾ oz/½ cup) of the rice in a small saucepan with enough water to cover by 1 cm (½ inch). Bring to the boil, cover with a lid and cook for 10 minutes or until the water is absorbed and the rice is plump. Remove from the heat and place in a bowl to cool.

Add the breadcrumbs, cooked rice and egg to the chorizo mixture, season with salt and pepper and mix well. Stuff the baby calamari with the mixture and secure the ends with toothpicks. Set aside.

Heat the remaining oil in a large deep-sided frying pan over high heat. Add the onions and garlic and cook until soft. Add the remaining 220 g (7¾ oz/1 cup) of rice to the pan and cook for a few minutes until the rice is slightly translucent. Deglaze the pan with the sherry and wine and stir well. Add the squid ink and fish stock, reduce the heat to low and cook for 15 minutes or until the rice is almost cooked. Season with nutmeg, fold in the butter, nestle the stuffed calamari in the rice and continue to cook for another few minutes until the calamari is just cooked and the rice is cooked. Remove the toothpicks from the calamari and divide the calamari between four shallow bowls, spoon over the rice, sprinkle on the nori shards, if using, and serve.

Note You can make this dish without the squid ink, if it is unavailable at your fishmongers.

100 ml (3½ fl oz) olive oil

2 large chorizo sausages, skin removed and meat finely diced

2 cuttlefish (about 200 g/7 oz each), cleaned and finely chopped

2 tablespoons chopped flat-leaf (Italian) parsley

1 long red chilli, seeded and finely chopped

330 g (11½ oz/1½ cups) arborio rice (or vialone rice)

30 g (1 oz/½ cup) fresh breadcrumbs

1 egg, beaten

8 baby calamari (about 80 g/ 2¾ oz each), cleaned

4 brown onions, finely diced

2 garlic cloves, sliced

100 ml (3½ fl oz) sherry (preferably Pedro Ximénez)

250 ml (9 fl oz/1 cup) sweet white wine

2 teaspoons squid ink (see note)

500 ml (17 fl oz/2 cups) fish stock

pinch of freshly grated nutmeg

2 tablespoons butter

2 sheets nori, fried, broken into shards (optional)

# TORTILLA DE CAMARONES AND PORK BELLY ON BRIOCHE BUNS

**The ability to make a good tortilla de camarones is one of the trademarks of a good cook in Spain—crunchy shellfish fritters that crumble in your mouth with every bite. They are very tasty, but can be very oily and messy. When I was eating them I kept thinking they would be great in a sandwich like pork crackling in a roast pork roll. And now I have it, I hope you enjoy it, too.**

Heat the olive oil in flameproof heavy-based saucepan or casserole dish over medium–high heat. Add the onions, garlic and carrots and cook for a few minutes to soften. Add the pork, sherry and enough water to cover. Bring to the boil, then reduce the heat, cover with a lid and cook for 2 hours until the pork is falling apart.

Meanwhile, to make the tortilla de camarone, mix the flour and eggs in a bowl. Add 100 ml (3½ fl oz) of water and stir to make a smooth batter. Add the spring onions, onion, parsley, dried shrimp and prawns. Season with salt, pepper and the paprika. Cover in plastic wrap and refrigerate for 30 minutes to rest.

Heat 2 tablespoons of olive oil in a frying pan over high heat. Spoon in 2 tablespoons of the batter, flatten with the back of a wooden spoon and cook for about 3 minutes until golden. Flip and cook the other side for the same length of time. Repeat with the remaining mixture to make 8 fritters. Drain on paper towel.

Remove the saucepan from the heat and transfer the pork to a warm platter. Leave to cook slightly and then roughly shred.

Mix the aioli in a bowl with the roasted garlic, lemon zest and juice. Fold through the red onion and parsley. Add the sherry vinegar.

Spread some garlic aioli on the base of each bun. Add some shredded pork then a tortilla de camarones fritter, top with the bun lid and serve immediately.

Note Dried shrimp are available from Asian supermarkets.
Look for the smallest school prawns you can find. Leave them unpeeled, for extra crunch—so the smaller the better.

2 tablespoons olive oil
2 brown onions, thinly sliced
4 garlic cloves
2 carrots, peeled and sliced
1 kg (2 lb 4 oz) pork belly
500 ml (17 fl oz/2 cups) Oloroso
    sherry
235 g (8½ oz/1 cup) aioli
    (or mayonnaise)
2 garlic cloves, roasted and smashed
zest and juice of 1 lemon
1 red onion, thinly sliced
handful flat-leaf (Italian) parsley,
    leaves picked
2 teaspoons sherry vinegar
8 small brioche or soft buns, halved
    and toasted

## Tortilla de camarones

75 g (2½ oz/½ cup) plain
    (all-purpose) flour
2 eggs
4 spring onions (scallions), finely
    chopped
1 brown onion, finely diced
2 tablespoons chopped flat-leaf
    (Italian) parsley
2 tablespoons dried shrimp
    (see note)
250 g (9 oz) small school prawns
    (shrimp—see note)
pinch of smoked paprika
olive oil, for shallow-frying

Cádiz

Preparation time: 20 minutes • Cooking time: 40 minutes • Serves: 4

# SALT-CRUSTED FRUITS OF THE SEA WITH JAMON AND SHERRY CREAM

Baking fish in salt is one of the most beautiful ways to enhance the natural sea-salt flavours naturally found in fish. It is a technique that is as old as the hills and, in the right restaurant, it can be the show-stopper of the night. I loved the theatre of breaking of the crust and wanted to do this at Maha. So I introduced a little sweet sherry and fennel to the original dish to help finesse the flavours of the fish. I know this is a little old school, but, hey, sometimes old school is the only school!

Preheat the oven to 200°C (400°F/Gas 6).

Put the olive oil and butter in a large saucepan over medium heat, to melt. Thinly slice one of the fennel bulbs and add to the pan with the onions and garlic. Cook for about 5 minutes until softened. Add the bay leaves and thyme, and season with salt and white pepper. Add the sherry and deglaze the pan, then bring to a gentle simmer for 2–3 minutes, stirring well until reduced. Add the cream and continue to cook for 6–8 minutes until thickened and reduced further. Check the seasoning. Remove from the heat and strain through a sieve into a bowl.

Divide the seafood between four 375 ml (13 fl oz/1½ cup) ovenproof ramekins, add the potatoes, remaining fennel bulbs, eel, jamon and parsley. Top with the sauce and season with plenty of salt and pepper. (See note.)

Divide the pastry sheet into four. Cut out rounds of the pastry and place on top of the ramekins. Brush with the beaten egg, season with salt, sprinkle over the paprika, then place in the oven and cook for 20 minutes or until the pastry is golden and crisp.

Remove from the oven and serve.

Note You don't need to fill the ramekins to the top. The gap between the pastry lid and the seafood allows it to cook quickly.

2 tablespoons olive oil
2½ tablespoons butter
5 small fennel bulbs
2 red onions, thinly sliced
2 garlic cloves, sliced
2 bay leaves
a few thyme sprigs
250 ml (9 fl oz/1 cup) dry sherry (such as Manzanilla or Fino)
500 ml (17 fl oz/2 cups) thickened (whipping) cream
1 kg (2 lb 4 oz) mixed fresh seafood (including clams/vongole, mussels, oysters, scallops, white-fleshed fish pieces)
4 small desiree or King Edward potatoes, peeled and boiled or roasted
½ smoked eel (about 200 g/7 oz), skin and bones removed
100 g (3½ oz) shaved jamon
4 tablespoons chopped flat-leaf (Italian) parsley
1 sheet puff pasty, thawed
1 egg yolk, beaten
pinch of smoked paprika

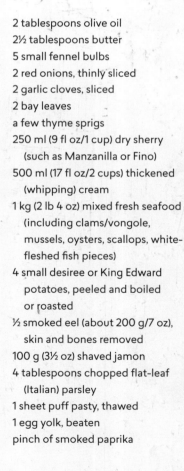

Preparation time: 10 minutes • Cooking time: 3 hours • Serves: 6–8

# BARBECUED PORK RIBS WITH FRIED EGGPLANT AND MOLASSES, AND SMOKED EGGPLANT DIP

Slow-cooked in a bitter and sweet sticky glaze would have to be one of the best ways to cook pork ribs, I think. I really enjoyed the way tapas bars would shallow-fry eggplant and then drizzle it in sugar cane molasses to offset the fatty oily flavour of the deep-fried eggplant and help cut through any oily flavours that might be left on your palate. It gave me the idea to glaze pork ribs in the same way to help cut and caramelise the pork fat, and the smoked eggplant dip rounds off the dish.

Preheat the oven to 150°C (300°F/Gas 2).

Mix the barbecue sauce and molasses together in a bowl then baste the pork ribs generously with half the sauce.

Place the ribs on a baking tray and cover tightly with foil. Bake for 2½ hours or until tender.

Meanwhile, to make the eggplant dip, cook the whole eggplant over a gas flame or barbecue grill for about 15 minutes until blackened and charred on all sides, turning with tongs. Remove from the heat and set aside to cool slightly. Peel the eggplant and discard the blackened skins. Place the flesh in a food processor with the tahini, garlic and lemon juice and blend until smooth. Drizzle in the olive oil and season with salt. Set aside.

Increase the oven temperature to 200°C (400°F/Gas 6), remove the foil from the ribs, baste again with some of the remaining molasses mixture and cook for about 15 minutes, until the ribs are sticky, dark and golden.

When the ribs are almost cooked, cut the Lebanese eggplant into large cubes and dust it with the flour.

Pour some canola oil into a deep frying pan, about 4 cm (1½ inches) deep, then heat over medium–high heat until it shimmers. If you have a kitchen thermometer, the oil will be ready when the temperature reaches 180°C (350°F). Alternatively, use a deep-fryer. Carefully add the eggplant and deep-fry for a few minutes until golden. Remove and drain on paper towel.

Put the deep-fried eggplant in a bowl and add the shallots, almonds, sherry vinegar, olive oil and remaining molasses mixture. Toss gently. Garnish with some parsley.

Remove the ribs from the oven and cut them either side of the bone. Scatter over the jamon slices and some parsley and serve with the fried eggplant and molasses, and the smoked eggplant dip.

250 ml (9 fl oz/1 cup) barbecue sauce
500 ml (17 fl oz/2 cups) sugar cane molasses, plus 2 teaspoons extra
1 kg (2 lb 4 oz) baby back pork ribs
2 Lebanese (long thin) eggplants (aubergines)
plain (all-purpose) flour, for dusting
canola oil, for deep-frying
2 French shallots, diced
2 tablespoons chopped toasted almonds
splash of sherry vinegar
drizzle of olive oil
flat-leaf (Italian) parsley leaves, to serve
jamon slices, to serve

## Smoked eggplant dip
2 eggplants (aubergines)
2 tablespoons tahini*
1 garlic clove
2 tablespoons lemon juice
60 ml (2 fl oz/¼ cup) olive oil
pinch of sea salt

# ORANGE BLOSSOM TOCINOS CIELO WITH PEAR SORBET, CLOVE POWDER AND YUZU

When I ate this dessert I couldn't believe how many egg yolks it had in it. It was full on! Then all of that sugar to finish it off with. Wow, it's a miracle that anyone in Seville has any teeth!

  I wanted to give it a go back at Maha, so I added a little orange blossom to remind me of all the orange trees that line the streets of Seville and I introduced a fresh pear sorbet to help cut the custard and add a little fresh fruit flavour.

## PEAR SORBET

Put the pears with their syrup in a food processor and blend until smooth. Place the purée and egg whites in the bowl of an electric stand mixer, attach the whisk attachment and whisk at moderate speed until the mixture doubles in size.

  Place the sugar and 100 ml (3½ fl oz) of water in a small saucepan over low heat and stir until the sugar has dissolved, then increase the heat, bring to the boil and cook to soft ball stage—to test if the syrup is ready drop a small amount into a shallow bowl of cold water to cool it down. If ready, it will form a soft ball. If you have a kitchen thermometer, the syrup will be ready when the temperature reaches 115–118°C (about 240°F).

  Decrease the speed to low and slowly pour in the syrup. Then whisk at high speed for 3 minutes or until cold. Transfer to a container and freeze overnight.

## ORANGE BLOSSOM TOCINOS CIELO

Preheat the oven to 150°C (300°F/Gas 2).

  Put 150 g (5½ oz/⅔ cup) of the caster sugar in a small saucepan over medium–low heat. Cook, stirring frequently, until it melts and becomes a light caramel. Pour into a 24 x 20 cm (9½ x 8 inch) ovenproof container and set aside.

  In a clean saucepan, combine the remaining caster sugar, the orange blossom water and 115 ml (3¾ fl oz) of water. Bring to the boil and cook until thickened—if you have a kitchen thermometer it wll be ready when the temperature reaches 104°C (220°F).

  Put the egg yolks in the bowl of an electric stand mixer with the whisk attachment and whisk at moderate–high speed to combine. Whisk in the sugar syrup and continue to whisk until cooled and thick.

  Pour the mixture over the caramel in the container. Place in a shallow baking dish and place in the oven. Carefully pour hot water into the baking dish to

### Pear sorbet
400 g (14 oz) tinned pears in syrup
3 egg whites
200 g (7 oz) caster (superfine) sugar

### Orange blossom tocinos cielo
400 g (14 oz) caster (superfine) sugar
2 tablespoons orange blossom water*
8 egg yolks

### Paprika meringue
6 large egg whites
140 g (5 oz) brown sugar
250 g (9 oz) caster (superfine) sugar
sweet paprika, for dusting

### Clove biscuit crumbs
125 g (4½ oz) almonds
300 g (10½ oz/2 cup) plain (all-purpose) flour
90 g (3¼ oz) caster (superfine) sugar
2 teaspoons ground cloves
1 teaspoon ground cinnamon
250 g (9 oz) butter, chilled and cubed
1 teaspoon natural vanilla extract

### Yuzu puree
350 ml (12 fl oz) yuzu juice
2 tablespoons gel cream

come halfway up the sides of the container. Place in the oven and bake for 30–40 minutes, until the custard is just set.

Carefully remove from the oven and from the water bath and allow to cool to room temperature. Cover with plastic wrap and refrigerate for 2 hours.

### PAPRIKA MERINGUE

Preheat the oven to 120°C (235°F/Gas ½). Line a baking tray with baking paper.

Place a saucepan of water over low heat and bring to a simmer. Place the egg whites, brown sugar and caster sugar in a heatproof bowl over the saucepan, ensuring the bowl doesn't come in contact with the water. Heat for approximately 5 minutes, or until a kitchen thermometer reaches 40°C (105°F).

Remove the mixture from the heat and place in the bowl of an electric stand mixer. Attach the whisk attachment and whisk at high speed for around 8 minutes, until the mixture has cooled.

Place spoonfuls of the mixture on the prepared tray, or use a piping (icing) bag, allowing room for the meringues to expand. Sprinkle over the paprika through a fine sieve. Place the tray in the oven and bake for 1¼ hours. When they are ready, the meringues will be dry underneath, but still soft in the centre.

Remove from the oven and allow to cool.

### CLOVE BISCUIT CRUMBS

Put the almonds in a food processor and process until finely ground. Add the flour, caster sugar, cloves and cinnamon, and process to combine. Add the butter and vanilla, and pulse to form a dough.

Divide the dough into four, then roll out each piece into 40 cm (16 inch) logs, wrap in plastic wrap, place on a tray and refrigerate for 30 minutes (the logs can be frozen at this stage).

When ready to bake, preheat the oven to 140°C (275°F/Gas 1).

Slice off 1 cm (½ inch) rounds, place on a baking tray lined with baking paper and bake for 20 minutes or until lightly coloured.

Remove from the oven and set aside to cool slightly.

To make the clove biscuit crumb, crumble the shortbread or process in a food processor.

### YUZU PURÉE

Put the yuzu juice in a bowl with the gel cream and combine using a hand-held stick blender until smooth and thickened.

### TO SERVE

Invert the orange blossom tocinos cielo on a flat dish and cut into squares. Serve with pear sorbet, some clove biscuit crumbs, yuzu purée and paprika meringue.

Note Cooking the custard in a water bath provides a gentle, even and consistent heat. Place the baking dish on the oven shelf before filling it with boiling water from the kettle. It is safer and easier and prevents spilling.

Orange blossom tocinos
cielo with pear sorbet,
clove powder and yuzu

# CORDOBA OLIVE OIL
# ICE CREAM

Every country I have travelled in has claimed to have the best olive oil in the world and, to be honest, up until recently I believed that back home in Australia we produced some killer oils to rival anything else going around. Well, I can honestly say that after tasting Venta del Baron oil from Spain it is the best I have ever experienced. I didn't want to mess with the grassy, fruity flavours of the oil, so I created this recipe to just complement the oil rather than overwhelm it.

You really do have to find the best olive oil possible for this dish. It just won't work with a poor quality olive oil. You do need an ice cream machine for this recipe.

Beat the sugar and egg yolks together in the bowl of an electric stand mixer with a whisk attachment for 5 minutes until pale in colour and thickened. Add the olive oil in a steady stream and continue beating for 3 minutes until smooth and airy. Add the milk, cream, vanilla seeds and salt and whisk until combined. Pour into an ice-cream machine and churn, then freeze according to the manufacturer's instructions.

Remove the ice cream from the freezer and leave to soften slightly before serving.

Note When making the custard base, ensure there are no lumps. Pass through a sieve to remove any lumps before churning. It is better to churn the ice cream when the custard is cool.

### Olive oil ice cream

220 g (7¾ oz/1 cup) sugar

6 egg yolks

80 ml (2½ fl oz/⅓ cup) olive oil (the best you can find)

750 ml (26 fl oz/3 cups) milk

250 ml (9 fl oz/1 cup) thickened (pouring) cream

1 vanilla bean, split and seeds scraped

1 teaspoon sea salt

# SMOKED CHIPOTLE AND CHOCOLATE FONDANT, PEDRO XIMENEZ AND ALMOND MILK ICE CREAM

Pedro Ximenez sherry and chocolate is one of the all-time classic matches. It just works. Pair that with a hot oozing chocolate fondant, a little kick from the smoked chipotle pepper and the soothing touch of the almond milk ice cream and you have all the makings of a knock-out dessert. And to be totally honest, my wife would kill me if I didn't put a fondant on the menu every year. So these ones are for you, Maha.

## ALMOND MILK ICE CREAM

Preheat the oven to 200°C (400°F/Gas 6). Place the almonds on a small baking tray. Roast for 5–10 minutes. Remove and steep in the milk in a large bowl in the fridge overnight. Blend together in a food processor until the texture is smooth.

Place the sugar and almond milk in a saucepan over low heat to dissolve the sugar and combine. Remove from the heat and set aside.

Beat the egg yolks in an electric stand mixer with the whisk attachment at moderate–high speed for 5 minutes until thick and pale. Add the almond milk mixture and whisk well to combine.

Whip the cream to soft peaks in the stand mixer with the whisk attachment. Fold the almond mixture into the cream. Pour into a container and freeze for 2–3 hours.

## PEDRO XIMÉNEZ POACHED FIGS

Put the sherry and sugar in a small saucepan over low heat and stir until the sugar has dissolved. Add the figs, cinnamon sticks, vanilla bean and orange zest, and simmer for 10 minutes or until the figs are soft. Add the almonds, then remove from the heat.

Serve immediately or keep refrigerated for up to 1 week.

### Almond milk ice cream
300 g (10½ oz) blanched almonds
500 ml (17 fl oz/2 cups) milk
100 g (3½ oz) caster (superfine) sugar
4 egg yolks
250 ml (9 fl oz/1 cup) thickened (whipping) cream

### Pedro Ximénez poached figs
250 ml (9 fl oz/1 cup) Pedro Ximénez sherry
250 g (9 oz) sugar
125 g (4½ oz/1 cup) dried white figs (or fresh figs when in season)
2 cinnamon sticks
1 vanilla bean, split and seeds scraped
zest of 1 orange
65 g (2¼ oz/½ cup) roughly chopped roasted almonds

### Smoked chipotle and bitter chocolate fondant
150 g (5½ oz) dark chocolate buttons
1 teaspoon dried chipotle chilli powder (see note)
150 g (5½ oz) butter, chopped, plus extra for greasing moulds
125 ml (2 fl oz/½ cup) pedro ximenez sherry
3 eggs
3 egg yolks
55 g (2 oz/¼ cup) caster (superfine) sugar
35 g (1¼ oz/¼ cup) plain (all-purpose) flour

## SMOKED CHIPOTLE AND BITTER CHOCOLATE FONDANT

Melt the chocolate buttons, chilli and butter, stirring occasionally, in the top of a double saucepan or in a heatproof bowl over simmering water until melted and glossy. Remove from the heat, add the pedro ximenex and stir to combine. Set aside.

Beat the eggs, egg yolks and sugar until thick and pale, sift in the flour stir in the chocolate mixture and mix gently to combine.

Grease six 125 ml (4 fl oz/½ cup) metal dariole moulds with butter. Pour the mixture into the moulds, cover with plastic wrap and refrigerate for 2 hours or up to 5 days.

Preheat the oven to 200°C (400°F/Gas 6).

When ready to serve, remove the plastic wrap, then place the moulds on a baking tray and bake for 10–12 minutes or until the puddings are firm around the edge. Remove from the oven and carefully run a knife around the edge of each mould, then turn the puddings out onto six plates.

## TO SERVE

Remove the almond ice cream from the freezer and leave to soften slightly.

Serve the fondants with the Pedro Ximenez poached figs and almond milk ice cream.

*Notes* Substitute tinned chipotles in adobo sauce if chipotle powder is unavailable.

The fondants need to be just cooked and still soft and molten in the centre. Check when cooking, the centre will still look uncooked and the outside will be just set.

Smoked chipotle and
chocolate fondant, pedro
ximenez and almond milk
ice cream

# PANTRY

**Argan oil** is a plant oil extract from the argan tree, which is native to Northern Africa. As well as being used in cooking it is also used as a personal-care product. It is available from health food shops, select supermarkets, as well as online.

**Aleppo pepper**, also known as pul biber, is a spice blend used in Middle Eastern cooking. It has a mild chilli taste and is available at specialist Middle Eastern grocery shops and online. If you can't find it, chilli flakes are a good substitute.

**Brik pastry** is available from specialty Middle Eastern grocery shops. If you have trouble finding it, use filo pastry instead.

**Capsicum paste** is available at specialty food stores. It can also be purchased online You can substitute a really good quality tomato paste.

**Harissa** is a North African hot chilli paste made from roasted red peppers and a combination of herbs and spices. It is available at specialty Middle Eastern grocery stores and select supermarkets, as well as online.

**Lamb tail fat** is available at butchers. Like other fats, it is solid at room temperature, but melts quickly with heat.

**Liquid glucose**, or glucose syrup, is a thick liquid sweetener made from starch. It is available at select supermarkets, as well as online.

**Pomegranate molasses** is the concentrated syrup of pomegranate juice. It is available at specialty Middle Eastern grocery stores and select supermarkets, as well as online.

**Preserved orange peel** is available at specialty Middle Eastern grocery stores and select supermarkets, as well as online. If you can't find it, use preserved lemon peel.

**Orange blossom water** is the distilled by-product of bitter-orange blossoms. It is available at specialty Middle Eastern grocery stores and select supermarkets, as well as online.

**Ras el hanout** is a North African spice mix that comprises of a variety of spices, such as cardamom and cumin. It is available at specialty Middle Eastern grocery stores and select supermarkets, as well as online.

**Sabaht baharat** (Lebanese 7 spice) is a Middle Eastern spice blend that usually consists of black pepper, cloves, cumin, nutmeg, coriander, cinnamon and smoked paprika. It is available at specialty Middle Eastern grocery stores and select supermarkets, as well as online.

**Saffron water** is made by adding a pinch of saffron and 1 teaspoon of saffron powder to 1 litre (35 fl oz/4 cups) of boiling water.

**Sucuk sausage** is a Turkish sausage, usually made with beef, spiced with paprika and fenugreek. It can be purchased from continental delicatessens and specialty Middle Eastern grocery shops.

**Sumac** is a Middle Eastern spice made from dried, ground berries of a wild bush. It is available at specialty Middle Eastern grocery stores, supermarkets, and online.

**Tahini** is a paste usually made from hulled sesame seeds. It can be found in the Middle Eastern section of supermarkets and specialty Middle Eastern grocery shops, as well as online.

**Za'atar** is a Middle Eastern spice blend that usually consists of thyme, sumac, marjoram, oregano, sesame seeds and salt. It is available at specialist Middle Eastern grocery shops and can also be purchased online. If you can't find it, thyme is a good substitute.

# INDEX

## A

Aleppo pepper 266
ali nazik lamb kofte with eggplant yoghurt and black bread garnish 123
almond milk ice cream 262
almond purée 226, 236
Andalucia, Spain 214–19
apple pastilla 202–3
apple and watercress dressing 225
arak-cured kingfish with smashed radish dressing 32
argan oil 190, 266
argan oil chocolate mud brownie with orange cinnamon ice cream 212
**artichokes**
artichoke and pea salad 242
roast Jerusalem artichokes 240

## B

baklava 64, 65
barbecued pork ribs with fried eggplant and molasses and smoked eggplant dip 255
**beans**
bissara with roasted garlic oil, scallops, carrots and cumin 171
broad bean salad 189
lamb shank kebab 116
**beef**
wagyu beef manti with peas, pickled onions and garlic yoghurt 136
wagyu beef with roasted cauliflower hummus and amlou dressing 190
wild greens with sucuk balls and eggs 131
beetroot mayonnaise 101
Beirut 26, 45
Bekaa Valley, Lebanon 54
bissara with roasted garlic oil, scallops, carrots and cumin 171
black bread 124
black bread garnish 123
black cabbage and hazelnut salad 150, 151
black garlic mayonnaise 150, 151
blackberry sorbet 154, 155
braised chickpea stew with lamb shin, eggplant and grains 175
braised lamb with saltbush and rockmelon 132
braised pig's ears, morcilla, quail eggs and jamon 236–7
braised rabbit with artichoke and pea salad 242–3
**bread**
black bread 124
black bread garnish 123
cumin flat bread 53
gremolata 186
nigella seed bread 82–3
pan-fried potato breads 182
preserved lemon and desert vegetable medfouna 194
taramasalata 105
brik pastry 266
broad bean salad 189
**burghul**
burghul dough 140
cracked wheat and tomato kibbeh 39
lamb and kishk kibbeh 42
burnt butter 140

## C

candied spiced pumpkin 61
capsicum paste 266
**caramel**
caramelised onion dressing 236
salted tahini caramel 64, 65
carob 58
carrots 171
carrot and preserved orange purée 193
sardine kefta with fresh chermoula salad 181
cauliflower: wagyu beef with roasted cauliflower hummus and amlou dressing 190
cemen-cured blue eye pastirma with taramasalata 105
**cheese**
feta borek 106
grilled haloumi with pomegranate and sumac dressing 35
morel, silverbeet and duck gozleme with morel butter 112
pastirma, prawn and feta pide 120
ricotta and carob lady fingers 58
chermoula paste 181
**chicken**
chicken cornbread dumpling soup 148
harira soup with pan-fried chicken dumplings and broad bean salad 189
quail egg kefta tabriz 81
saffron marinated chicken 172
stuffed chicken wings with sour cherry barbecue sauce 45
**chickpeas**
braised chickpea stew with lamb shin, eggplant and grains 175
hummus 53
quail egg kefta tabriz 81
roast chickpea hummus with lamb kebab 139
wagyu beef with roasted cauliflower hummus and amlou dressing 190
**chilli**
eggplant pickle with black pepper and green chilli 76
smoked chipotle and chocolate fondant, Pedro

Ximenez and almond milk ice cream 262–3
chips, spicy Dahlia 46
**chocolate**
argan oil chocolate mud brownie with orange cinnamon ice cream 212
chocolate and pistachio m'hencha 206
salted white chocolate ice cream 211
smoked chipotle and chocolate fondant, Pedro Ximenez and almond milk ice cream 262–3
cinnamon sugar 65
clementine and saffron marmalade 199
clove biscuit crumbs 256, 257
Cordoba olive oil ice cream 260
cornbread 150
cornbread and fennel seed crumbed sardines 144
**couscous**
foot of the mountain couscous with garden vegetables 178
shellfish moghrabieh 36
cracked wheat and tomato kibbeh 39
cumin flat bread 53
cured salmon with beetroot mayonnaise, pumpkin purée and fennel vinaigrette 101

## D

spicy Dahlia chips 46
date, orange and olive oil cake with salted white chocolate ice cream 211
date and ras el hanout ice cream 202
desserts see sweet things
dip, smoked eggplant 255
doughnuts, pistachio and barberry nougat, with orange blossom syrup 90
**dressings**
apple and watercress dressing 225
beetroot mayonnaise 101
black garlic mayonnaise 150, 151
caramelised onion dressing 236
fennel vinaigrette 101
garlic yoghurt 136, 140
gazpacho-flavoured mayonnaise 230
harissa aioli 222
herbed crème fraîche 147
mustard mayonnaise 16, 17
preserved lemon dressing 109
roast garlic vinaigrette 87
sherry dressing 227
smashed radish dressing 32
smoked eel dressing 102
smoked eggplant mayonnaise 106
**duck**
duck awarma 50
duck fat 50
freekeh risotto with duck awarma, poached eggs and toasted nuts 54

hummus with duck awarma and cumin flat
   breads 53
morel, silverbeet and duck gozleme with morel
   butter 112
tea-smoked duck with black cabbage and
   hazelnut salad 150–1

**dumplings**
chicken cornbread dumpling soup 148
harira soup with pan-fried chicken dumplings
   and broad bean salad 189

# E

**eggplant**
ali nazik lamb kofte with eggplant yoghurt and
   black bread garnish 123
barbecued pork ribs with fried eggplant and
   molasses and smoked eggplant dip 255
braised chickpea stew with lamb shin, eggplant
   and grains 175
eggplant pickle with black pepper and green
   chilli 76
lamb shoulder with potato and eggplant tagine
   186
smoked eggplant mayonnaise 106

**eggs**
braised pig's ears, morcilla, quail eggs and jamon
   236–7
freekeh risotto with duck awarma, poached eggs
   and toasted nuts 54
pickled quail eggs 226
quail egg kefta tabriz 81
wild greens with sucuk balls and eggs 131

# F

fennel vinaigrette 101
fenugreek salad 87
feta borek 106

**figs**
fig and walnut ice cream 62
Pedro Ximenez poached figs 262
vine leaf wrapped quail, sucuk and candied
   walnuts and figs 127

**fish**
arak-cured kingfish with smashed radish dressing
   32
cemen-cured blue eye pastirma with
   taramasalata 105
cornbread and fennel seed crumbed sardines
   144
cured salmon with beetroot mayonnaise,
   pumpkin purée and fennel vinaigrette 101
sardine kefta with fresh chermoula salad 181
sardine and preserved orange rice pilaf with
   herbed crème fraîche 147

smoked trout trahana 115
taramasalata 105
tartare of tuna, harissa aioli 222
*see also seafood*
foot of the mountain couscous with garden
   vegetables 178

**freekeh**
braised chickpea stew with lamb shin, eggplant
   and grains 175
freekeh risotto with duck awarma, poached eggs
   and toasted nuts 54
frozen peanut butter parfait, salted tahini caramel
   and broken baklava 64–5

# G

Gallipoli Campaign 96
garden vegetables with foot of the mountain
   couscous 178

**garlic**
black garlic mayonnaise 150, 151
braised lamb with saltbush and rockmelon 132
eggplant pickle with black pepper and green
   chilli 76
garlic yoghurt 136, 140
lamb shank kebab 116
roast garlic vinaigrette 87
slow-roasted lamb shoulder 82
garnish, black bread 123
gazpacho-flavoured mayonnaise 230
glucose syrup 266
gozleme dough 112
gremolata 186

# H

haloumi, grilled, with pomegranate and sumac
   dressing 35
harira soup with pan-fried chicken dumplings and
   broad bean salad 189
harissa 266
harissa aioli 222
herbed crème fraîche 147
hummus 53
roast chickpea hummus with lamb kebab 139
roasted cauliflower hummus 190

# I

**ice cream**
almond milk ice cream 262
Cordoba olive oil ice cream 260
date and ras el hanout ice cream 202
fig and walnut ice cream 62
orange cinnamon ice cream 212
salted white chocolate ice cream 211
icli kofte with garlic yoghurt and burnt butter 140

Iran 68–73
Istanbul 96

# J

Jerusalem artichokes, roast 240

# K

kangaroo de toro with roast Jerusalem artichokes
   240

**kebab**
lamb shank kebab 116
roast chickpea hummus with lamb kebab 139

**kefta**
quail egg kefta tabriz 81
sardine kefta with fresh chermoula salad 181

**kibbeh**
cracked wheat and tomato kibbeh 39
lamb and kishk kibbeh 42

**kofte**
ali nazik lamb kofte with eggplant yoghurt and
   black bread garnish 123
icli kofte with garlic yoghurt and burnt butter 140

# L

**lamb**
ali nazik lamb kofte with eggplant yoghurt and
   black bread garnish 123
braised chickpea stew with lamb shin, eggplant
   and grains 175
braised lamb with saltbush and rockmelon 132
lamb and kishk kibbeh 42
lamb sfiha 57
lamb shank kebab 116
lamb shoulder with potato and eggplant tagine
   186
lamb tail fat 266
quail egg kefta tabriz 81
roast chickpea hummus with lamb kebab 139
slow-roasted lamb shoulder with nomad's
   jewelled yoghurt and nigella seed bread 82–3
wild greens with sucuk balls and eggs 131
Lebanese 7 spice 266
Lebanon 24–7

**lemon**
preserved lemon and desert vegetable
   medfouna 194
preserved lemon dressing 109

# M

Maha 6
Malta 10–15, 96
manti dough 136
marmalade, clementine and saffron 199
Marrakesh 167

mastic pudding with chocolate soil, blackberry
    sorbet and rosemary pearls 154–5
meat curing 105
melon: braised lamb with saltbush and rockmelon
    132
mint and apple pastilla with date and ras el hanout
    ice cream 202–3
mint crème 202
Moorish chilled almond and orange blossom soup
    with apple and watercress dressing 225
morel, silverbeet and duck gozleme with morel
    butter 112
Morocco 162–7, 216
mustard mayonnaise 16, 17

**N**

nigella seed bread 82–3
nomad's jewelled yoghurt 82
nougat, pistachio and barberry 90

**O**

olive oil poached potatoes, pickled octopus and
    green olives 235
**onions**
    caramelised onion dressing 236
    couscous with onion 36
    kangaroo de toro 240
    lamb kebabs 139
    red onion salad 139
**orange**
    clementine and saffron marmalade 199
    date, orange and olive oil cake with salted white
        chocolate ice cream 211
    orange blossom syrup 90
    orange blossom tocinos cielo with pear sorbet,
        clove powder and yuzu 256–7
    orange blossom water 266
    orange cinnamon ice cream 212
    orange and coriander crumb 102
    orange grove beghrir with orange blossom
        yoghurt 200
    preserved orange peel 266
    sardine and preserved orange rice pilaf with
        herbed crème fraîche 147
Ottoman Empire 96

**P**

pan-fried potato breads 182
paprika meringue 256, 257
pastirma, prawn and feta pide 120
pastizzi 16, 17
    pork and pea pastizzi with mustard mayonnaise
        16–17
**pastry**
    chocolate and pistachio m'hencha 206
    gozleme 112
    mint and apple pastilla with date and ras el
        hanout ice cream 202–3

pastirma, prawn and feta pide 120
ricotta and carob lady fingers 58
salt-crusted fruits of the sea with jamon and
    sherry cream 252
peaches, saffron roasted, with saffron fairy floss 93
peanut butter parfait 64
pear sorbet 256
**peas**
    artichoke and pea salad 242
    pork and pea pastizzi with mustard mayonnaise
        16–17
Persian food 70, 73
**pickles**
    eggplant pickle with black pepper and green chilli 76
    pickled octopus 235
pide, pastirma, prawn and feta 120
pistachio and barberry nougat doughnuts with
    orange blossom syrup 90
pistachio crumble 158
poached lobster pringa with gazpacho-flavoured
    mayonnaise and prawn crackling 230
pomegranate molasses 266
**pork**
    barbecued pork ribs with fried eggplant and
        molasses and smoked eggplant dip 255
    braised pig's ears, morcilla, quail eggs and jamon
        236–7
    pork and pea pastizzi with mustard mayonnaise
        16–17
    roasted pork belly with fenugreek salad and roast
        garlic vinaigrette 87
    tortilla de camarones and pork belly on brioche
        buns 249
**potatoes**
    lamb shoulder with potato and eggplant tagine
        186
    olive oil poached potatoes, pickled octopus
        and green olives 235
    pan-fried potato breads 182
    quail egg kefta tabriz 81
    spicy Dahlia chips 46
**prawns**
    Moorish chilled almond and orange blossom
        soup with apple and watercress dressing 225
    pastirma, prawn and feta pide 120
    preserved lemon and desert vegetable medfouna
        194
preserved lemon dressing 109
preserved orange peel 266
**pumpkin**
    candied spiced pumpkin 61
    pumpkin purée 101
    pumpkin Turkish delight 161

**Q**

quail eggs
    braised pig's ears, morcilla, quail eggs and jamon
        236–7

pickled quail eggs 226
quail egg kefta tabriz 81
quail, sucuk and candied walnuts and figs, vine leaf
    wrapped 127

**R**

**rabbit**
    braised rabbit with artichoke and pea salad
        242–3
    rabbit stew with sultana gremolata 21
radish: smashed radish dressing 32
ras el hanout 266
red onion salad 139
rfissa 172
**rice**
    braised chickpea stew with lamb shin, eggplant
        and grains 175
    rosewater sutlac with pistachio crumble 158
    sardine and preserved orange rice pilaf with
        herbed crème fraîche 147
    squid ink rice with chorizo-filled baby calamari
        and seaweed 246
    stuffed mussels with preserved lemon dressing
        109
    vine leaf wrapped quail, sucuk and candied
        walnuts and figs 127
ricotta and carob lady fingers 58
risotto, freekeh, with duck awarma, poached eggs
    and toasted nuts 54
roast chickpea hummus with lamb kebab 139
roasted pork belly with fenugreek salad and roast
    garlic vinaigrette 87
rosemary pearls 154
rosewater sutlac with pistachio crumble 158

**S**

sabaht baharat 266
saffron 93
    clementine and saffron marmalade 199
    saffron marinated chicken 172
    saffron roasted peaches with saffron fairy floss
        93
    saffron water 266
    veal shin and saffron with carrot and preserved
        orange purée 193
**salads**
    artichoke and pea salad 242
    black cabbage and hazelnut salad 150, 151
    broad bean salad 189
    fenugreek salad 87
    fresh chermoula salad 181
    red onion salad 139
salmorejo with jamon, quail egg, green apple and
    sherry dressing 226–7
salt-crusted fruits of the sea with jamon and sherry
    cream 252
salted white chocolate ice cream 211
sardine kefta with fresh chermoula salad 181

sardine and preserved orange rice pilaf with herbed crème fraîche 147

scallop-filled zucchini flowers with smoked eel dressing and orange and coriander crumb 102

**seafood**
bissara with roasted garlic oil, scallops, carrots and cumin 171
Moorish chilled almond and orange blossom soup with apple and watercress dressing 225
olive oil poached potatoes, pickled octopus and green olives 235
pastirma, prawn and feta pide 120
poached lobster pringa with gazpacho-flavoured mayonnaise and prawn crackling 230
salt-crusted fruits of the sea with jamon and sherry cream 252
scallop-filled zucchini flowers with smoked eel dressing and orange and coriander crumb 102
shellfish moghrabieh 36
smoked eel dressing 102
squid ink rice with chorizo-filled baby calamari and seaweed 246
stuffed mussels with preserved lemon dressing 109
tortilla de camarones and pork belly on brioche buns 249
*see also fish*

salted tahini caramel 64, 65

semolina: orange grove beghrir with orange blossom yoghurt 200

shellfish moghrabieh 36

sherry dressing 227

silverbeet
morel, silverbeet and duck gozleme with morel butter 112
wild greens with sucuk balls and eggs 131

slow-roasted lamb shoulder with nomad's jewelled yoghurt and nigella seed bread 82–3

smashed radish dressing 32

smoked chipotle and chocolate fondant, Pedro Ximenez and almond milk ice cream 262–3

smoked eel dressing 102

smoked eggplant dip 255

smoked eggplant mayonnaise 106

smoked trout trahana 115

**soup**
chicken cornbread dumpling soup 148
harira soup with pan-fried chicken dumplings and broad bean salad 189
Moorish chilled almond and orange blossom soup with apple and watercress dressing 225

sour cherry barbecue sauce 45

spiced wafer 222

squid ink rice with chorizo-filled baby calamari and seaweed 246

stuffed chicken wings with sour cherry barbecue sauce 45

stuffed mussels with preserved lemon dressing 109

sucuk sausage 266
vine leaf wrapped quail, sucuk and candied walnuts and figs 127
wild greens with sucuk balls and eggs 131

sugar syrup 161

sultana gremolata 21

sumac 266

**sweet things**
argan oil chocolate mud brownie with orange cinnamon ice cream 212
chocolate and pistachio m'hencha 206
Cordoba olive oil ice cream 260
date, orange and olive oil cake with salted white chocolate ice cream 211
date and ras el hanout ice cream 202
fig and walnut ice cream 62
frozen peanut butter parfait, salted tahini caramel and broken baklava 64–5
mastic pudding with chocolate soil, blackberry sorbet and rosemary pearls 154–5
mint and apple pastilla with date and ras el hanout ice cream 202–3
mint crème 202
orange blossom tocinos cielo with pear sorbet, clove powder and yuzu 256–7
paprika meringue 256, 257
pistachio and barberry nougat doughnuts with orange blossom syrup 90
pumpkin Turkish delight 161
rosewater sutlac with pistachio crumble 158
saffron roasted peaches with saffron fairy floss 93
smoked chipotle and chocolate fondant, Pedro Ximenez and almond milk ice cream 262–3

**T**
tahini 266
taramasalata 105
tartare of tuna, harissa aioli 222
tea-smoked duck with black cabbage and hazelnut salad 150–1
tempura batter 109
**tomatoes**
cracked wheat and tomato kibbeh 39
lamb and kishk kibbeh 42
lamb shank kebab 116
salmorejo purée 226
tortilla de camarones and pork belly on brioche buns 249
Turkey 94–9

**V**
veal shin and saffron with carrot and preserved orange purée 193
**vegetables**
foot of the mountain couscous with garden vegetables 178
preserved lemon and desert vegetable medfouna 194

vegetable stock 178

village-style feta borek with smoked eggplant mayonnaise 106

vine leaf wrapped quail, sucuk and candied walnuts and figs 127

**W**
wagyu beef manti with peas, pickled onions and garlic yoghurt 136
wagyu beef with roasted cauliflower hummus and amlou dressing 190
**walnuts**
fig and walnut ice cream 62
gremolata 186
lamb shank kebab 116
vine leaf wrapped quail, sucuk and candied walnuts and figs 127
wild greens with sucuk balls and eggs 131

**Y**
**yoghurt**
eggplant yoghurt 123
garlic yoghurt 136, 140
nomad's jewelled yoghurt 82
orange grove beghrir with orange blossom yoghurt 200
yuzu purée 256, 257

**Z**
za'atar 266
zucchini flowers, scallop-filled, with smoked eel dressing and orange and coriander crumb 102

Published in 2016 by Murdoch Books, an imprint of Allen & Unwin

Murdoch Books Australia
83 Alexander Street
Crows Nest NSW 2065
Phone: +61 (0) 2 8425 0100
Fax: +61 (0) 2 9906 2218
murdochbooks.com.au
info@murdochbooks.com.au

Murdoch Books UK
Erico House, 6th Floor
93–99 Upper Richmond Road
Putney, London SW15 2TG
Phone: +44 (0) 20 8785 5995
murdochbooks.co.uk
info@murdochbooks.co.uk

For Corporate Orders & Custom Publishing contact Noel Hammond,
National Business Development Manager, Murdoch Books Australia

Publisher: Jane Morrow
Design Manager: Megan Pigott
Designer: Jacqui Porter
Editor: Emma Hutchinson
Food Editor and Stylist: Caroline Velik
Photographer: Rob Palmer
Food Preparation: Petros Dellidis
Production Manager: Alexandra Gonzalez

A cataloguing-in-publication entry is available from the catalogue of the National Library of Australia at nla.gov.au.

ISBN 978 1 74336 720 9 Australia
ISBN 978 1 74336 733 9 UK

A catalogue record for this book is available
from the British Library.

Colour reproduction by Splitting Image Colour Studio Pty Ltd, Clayton, Victoria
Printed by 1010 Printing International Limited, China

IMPORTANT: Those who might be at risk from the effects of salmonella poisoning (the elderly, pregnant women, young children and those suffering from immune deficiency diseases) should consult their doctor with any concerns about eating raw eggs.

OVEN GUIDE: You may find cooking times vary depending on the oven you are using. For fan-forced ovens, as a general rule, set the oven temperature to 20°C (35°F) lower than indicated in the recipe.

MEASURES GUIDE: We have used 20 ml (4 teaspoon) tablespoon measures. If you are using a 15 ml (3 teaspoon) tablespoon add an extra teaspoon of the ingredient for each tablespoon specified.